LAYERED MONEY

MONEY

FROM GOLD AND DOLLARS TO BITCOIN AND
CENTRAL BANK DIGITAL CURRENCIES

NIK BHATIA

*This book is dedicated to my wife and life partner
Chandni and our sweetheart daughter Ria Tara*

CONTENTS

PREFACE

W E STAND TODAY FACING AN INTERNATIONAL MONETARY system on the precipice of overhaul, something that rarely occurs. This book was written to provide a topography of money at these uncertain crossroads. Maps help us navigate geographies and terrains, but until now they have never been associated with money. This book provides a map of our financial system throughout time, and a preview of what the map of digital money will look like in the future. It endows the reader with a new framework called *layered money* to describe our evolving monetary system, help us navigate the geomorphology of money, and explain how different forms of money relate to each other.

By tracing the evolution of layered money, we gain a fascinating perspective on how and why humans interact with their chosen currencies. Along with dissecting the progression of currency, this book tackles a key question: what does the future of money entail? Many will say "it's digital," but to most of us, money already seems digital. We use smartphone applications to manage checking accounts and make contactless payments and are increasingly surrendering to a cashless existence. But now that Bitcoin has captivated the world's monetary imagination, *digital money* has taken on a whole new meaning.

Part of the reason for this ambiguity is that monetary science, or the study of money, lacks the proper vernacular and theoretical framework to incorporate Bitcoin; it desperately needs a fresh update to include this novel form of money. Updates to monetary science are extremely rare, and in order to explain the enormous one about to occur, we have to look at its past to properly contextualize Bitcoin's impact on the future of money. And the update is well worth it; Bitcoin and its many iterations provide the fresh start in transparency and choice the world needs as we face the next iteration of money.

This book is an attempt to understand and explain how this integration of Bitcoin will occur, and how it will change the fate of our monetary system. In order to do that, we need a more accessible way to understand monetary science itself, which historically has been shrouded in doctorate level economic theory—very few truly understand where money comes from, or what a monetary system even is. The goal of this book is to reframe our monetary system for the uninitiated and explain it from the beginning.

Most importantly, readers will come away with an understanding that money is a layered system. Using original *layered* terminology, this book will explain why human beings began using monetary systems instead of coins, how these systems evolved, and how complicated and multilayered they have become today. Readers should be able to use this book to understand on which layer of money their assets are located and navigate between the layers of money. In a future world of currency choice, being able to navigate the monetary map will be empowering.

Layered Money Demonstrated

Before beginning the saga of layered money, it's best to provide the reader with a brief example and illustration of the framework. The most basic example of this new terminology can be demonstrated by examining the relationship between a gold coin and a gold certificate from 1928 in the United States of America. In this example, the gold certificate has the following phrase written on it:

> *This certifies that there have been deposited in the Treasury of the United States of America ten dollars in gold coin payable to the bearer on demand*

Let's interpret this statement by using the layered terminology. First-layer money, a gold coin, is held in a vault. Second-layer money, a gold certificate, is printed and circulated in place of the gold coin. The paper has value to whoever is holding the piece of paper itself, called the bearer. Both the coin and the certificate are forms of money, but they are qualitatively different from each other. This relationship between two layers of money (Figure 2) is another way to describe a balance sheet of assets and liabilities (Figure 1).

UNITED STATES TREASURY BALANCE SHEET	
Assets	*Liabilities*
Gold coins	Gold certificates

Figure 1

Figure 2

If we diligently apply this new framework to monetary science and trace it back to its beginnings, the yarn that unravels is a comprehensive history of money. As core players in the international monetary system begin to announce their forthcoming digital currencies, we urgently require a lucid way to analyze the coming changes, but we can't easily do so within the current mainstream financial terminology. This book frames money as a layered system because it's a clearer way to conceptualize the changes coming to our financial system, a system that temporarily erupts in chaos every few years only to be calmed by increasing amounts of government and central bank intervention.

There is a path to a more stable future; this book prescribes one that relies heavily on technological innovations that have merged monetary science with another previously unrelated science: cryptography. With its pervasive spread throughout minds and markets across the world since 2009, the science of cryptography is forcing the financial world to abandon old systems for new ones, much like the Internet has done to countless industries since the turn of this millennium. These new systems need to be carefully imagined, and we'll use this new layered framework to explain how it all might unfold. What is the role of non-government currencies in our future? Will Bitcoin coexist with government currencies or replace them? The answers mandate a study of layered money. It begins with a gold coin created in 1252.

CHAPTER 1

FIORINO D'ORO
(FLORIN OF GOLD)

I and my companions suffer from a disease of the heart which can be cured only with gold.
—HERNÁN CORTÉS

BEFORE LAYERED MONEY, THERE WAS SIMPLY MONEY. FOR our species, money is a tool that allowed us to progress away from reciprocal altruism, wherein animals swap favors, like when monkeys groom each other.[1] Some prefer to call money a shared illusion, although the word illusion implies that all forms of money lack basis in reality. It's better to say, instead, that some forms of money are shared illusions, and others might prove to be real over a long enough time horizon.

Humans used seashells, animal teeth, jewelry, livestock, and iron tools as tokens of barter for tens of thousands of years, but eventually settled on gold and silver in the past few millennia as globally accepted forms of currency. Something about these two chemical elements exuded preciousness, and humans anointed them as the quintessential money. This anointment was responsible for a tremendous advance in the

---

[1] *Szabo*

globalization of human civilization, as precious metals provided improved ways to preserve generational wealth and facilitate trade between complete strangers in different corners of the planet.

Selecting what was to be used as money wasn't always easy. Shells might have been perfect for trade a thousand miles from the ocean but were plentiful by the seashore for others and thus not a great tool for storing value across generations and continents. Iron tools were highly valuable for hunting and weaponry and could hold value for centuries but weren't necessarily the best circulating medium because they lacked portability and divisibility, unlike shells. Precious metals worked well in both capacities and gradually became universally agreed upon as the best form of money.

Money isn't only used as a medium of exchange and a store of value; it's also a counting system. It's a way of listing prices, tallying revenue, calculating profits, and bringing the entire array of economic activity under one accounting denomination. The Latin root of the word denomination is *nomin*, or name. Religious denominations are a way for people to name their particular religious beliefs, just as accounting denominations are a way for people to name their revenues, expenses, and profits. When people come together to agree on a unified accounting denomination, pricing goods and services becomes easier because everybody is on the same page as to what is considered money. When everybody can *name* their price in the same terms, economic activity flourishes.

Denominating merely in gold wasn't enough though. Trade using gold jewelry, bars, and nuggets stipulated constant measurement of weight and purity, making an unspecified gold denomination not very useful. This chapter will show how coins solved this problem by introducing weights, purities, and trustworthiness.

The First Coins

The father of history, Greek historian Herodotus, traced the first signs of gold and silver coins to Lydia, modern-day Turkey, around 700 BC. Evidence of gold and silver jewelry being used as money goes back tens of thousands of years, but the arrival of the coin transformed these precious metals into proper accounting denominations. The coins of Lydia were embossed with an image of a roaring lion and weighed 126 grains, which is about 8 grams. Because all coins had a precise amount of gold, they could then be used as a unit of account. Today, uniformly weighted coins might seem like the obvious form of gold and silver money, but precious metals carried a global aura of currency for thousands of years before the first Lydian coin was created. With consistent weights, coins were a revolution in simplicity and changed money forever. They eliminated the need to weigh and test the purity of every piece of metal before two parties could transact, and this seemingly straightforward adaptation ultimately transformed the world of trade.

What were some of the most important characteristics of coins, and why were they so revolutionary as a form of money? First and most importantly, coins were made with metals that were considered precious, durable, and rare. Gold and silver had a proven track record of thousands of years as money, so having coins struck from these two metals assured that they would have natural demand. If the coins were made of stone, for example, they would have no such demand, because common rocks aren't precious or rare.

The next characteristic of coins that truly brought a leap forward in both money and human civilization was the idea of fungible, or interchangeable, money. When two things are *fungible*, they have equal and undifferentiated value between them, like how we think of a one-dollar bill as being equal to any other one-dollar bill. Coins coming from the same mint were all identical, eliminating the burdensome measurement process from everyday transactions. Coins were a huge advancement in the measurability of money, especially when compared to gold bricks of non-uniform weights and gold jewelry with unspecified purities. Coin uniformity and fungibility made them perfect accounting denominations, allowing societies the powerful tool of being able to measure everything in one unit.

Money should also be divisible: for example, livestock being used as currency dates back thousands of years, but cattle aren't divisible and therefore are useless in small transactions. Coins were perfect for divisibility: they each represented a small amount of value and could be used in the smallest transactions whilst also easily amassed for larger ones.

Lastly, the best coins were the ones that were difficult to forge. Counterfeiting could seriously undermine the value of a currency, so mints had to create coins with difficult-to-mimic engravings. If coins circulating were thought to be real, and people believed that counterfeits were unlikely to exist, this would allow people to transact with each other without the burden of auditing every coin for authenticity.

Government Influence Over Money

Worldwide demand for coins boomed due to their economic advancement, and governments became the largest supplier. Rulers found it impossible to resist immortalizing themselves, minting coins in their names engraved with their faces to circulate as money within their borders. This wasn't, however, purely a form of regal vanity. Coin mints gave governments the power to use money to their own benefit, leading to lasting societal impact and the rise and fall of empires.

The Roman Empire gives us a perfect example of how coins led to government influence over currency. In the first century AD, shortly after the beginning of the Roman Empire, coins called *denarii* (plural for *denarius*) were minted by the government in Rome, and due to the empire's worldwide expanse were used across Europe, Asia, and Africa. For the first time, global monetary standards evolved based on precious metal coins minted by a single entity. The influence of the powerful Roman Empire's currency denomination stemmed from its imperial dominance and reverberated throughout the world. Coins named *dinar* would surface from India to Egypt to Spain for centuries thereafter.[2]

In the second century under the rule of Marcus Aurelius, the denarius coin weighed about 3.4 grams and contained about 80% silver, which was already a reduction from its

---

2 *Bundesbank*

98% purity when Augustus Caesar declared himself the first Emperor of Rome three centuries prior. Throughout the ages, currencies have ceased to exist because of one rudimentary fact: governments are unable to resist the temptation to create free money for themselves. The case of Roman currency devaluation was no exception. When the Roman Empire reduced the precious metal content of the denarius while leaving its name and value unchanged, it essentially had created money for itself; each denarius had a higher purity than its successor. This act of cheapening money by the government reduces trust in the currency and leads to unstable prices and societal vulnerability. By the end of the third century, the denarius had been devalued so frequently that its purity was down to only 5% silver, corresponding with the Crisis of the Third Century, a period in which several Emperors were assassinated and the Roman Empire almost collapsed. Currency devaluation was a trend that persisted throughout the world, making what happened in thirteenth century Florence so remarkable.

The Florin

The northern Italian cities of Florence, Venice, Genoa, and Pisa established themselves as city-republics after breaking free from their feudal overlords during the eleventh century, and their newfound independence was later followed by the coinage of their own money. In the year 1252, when the Florentine mint struck the first *Fiorino d'Oro*, or gold *florin*, nothing novel had necessarily been accomplished. It was merely another coin. However, as decades and centuries passed without a change in the coin's gold weight and purity, the florin earned a reputation that eventually drove all those surrounding it into its denomination. Historically, precious metal coins were durable, divisible, and portable, but with governments constantly reducing the purity of their coins, no coin existed with multigenerational credibility. The Florentine mint changed that. The florin maintained an unchanged weight and purity, about 3.5 grams of pure gold, spanning an astounding four centuries. By the time the florin denomination was one hundred years old, it had evolved into the international monetary standard for pan-European finance. High salaries, jewelry, real estate, and capital investment were all priced in florin.[3] It also found popularity amongst working people as a way to literally carry their entire life's savings in their pocket. Florins proved to be exemplary collateral and could easily be pawned to borrow silver coins for smaller transactions. The florin as a unit of account disseminated throughout Europe and beyond as the world's most trusted and stable monetary denomination. The extraordinary stability of the florin alone didn't drive monetary innovation during the Renaissance, but its multi-century popularity coincided with simultaneous advancements in mathematics, accounting, and banking that resulted in a prodigious transformation of the human experience with money. Before detailing these progressions, we first have to understand the flaws in coin-money they addressed.

---

3   *Goldthwaite*

Coin Multiplicity

Coinage alone did not make a monetary system. Coin-money presented two enormous problems for the global economy, which in that period consisted of cities in Europe, northern Africa, and the Middle East connected by the Mediterranean Sea. There were simply too many different currencies, and this problem of coin multiplicity severely hampered money velocity.

Money velocity measures how quickly money changes hands. It's the speed at which money moves from one owner to the next, and only with sufficient speed can money help human beings trade to their fullest potential. Gold and silver coins accelerated money velocity relative to more primitive ages when precious metal bars and nuggets of non-standardized weights were used as mediums of exchange. But a world of coin multiplicity where thousands of competing coins were used meant that an equivalency conversion had to occur alongside practically every single transaction between people of different geographies. This presented major challenges to unlocking the next levels of money velocity and international trade, because standards for weights and purities varied wildly across the world.

Money changers specialized in this requisite conversion and became integral to all trade. They were tasked with trafficking between hundreds or even thousands of different coins in order to facilitate every type of international exchange. A lack of coin uniformity throughout the world allowed money changers to profit any instance a merchant or customer needed conversion from one currency to another. This profession still exists today in the form of foreign exchange brokers, or those that convert Mexican *pesos* to Brazilian *real*, for example.

Compounding the coin multiplicity problem was the issue of *bimetallism*, which allows for two separate metals to be used as money. Silver is a more abundant metal in the Earth's crust than gold is and has historically served as the money of common people and daily transactions. Gold, on the contrary, is the more desired precious metal and sought-after form of wealth, but it didn't suffice for daily use: a single florin was worth more than a week of labor from the average worker.[4] The gold and silver dichotomy complicated the formation of a unified monetary system until the end of the nineteenth century.

Risks of Physical Transfer

The second major challenge of a coin-money system was the risk associated with the physical transfer of coins. Sending coins across land and sea was perilous and a logistical nightmare during the medieval era. Shipwrecks were often the unfriendly collateral damage of trying to settle international debts. Part of the reason precious metals were deemed precious was their indestructibility, so it would seem apt that an entire industry of shipwreck hunting exists today to find gold and silver coins that were lost during this era.

The solution to these problems was the idea of deferred settlement. As an alternative to the physical transfer of metal, *deferred settlement* takes place when one party unambiguously

---

4   Goldthwaite

promises to pay another at a later time. At that time, *final settlement* occurs, and the owed party receives ultimate payment, historically gold and silver. These promises, or credits, were made as a way for merchants to reduce the risk of international coin transfer. These types of deferred settlement arrangements existed long before the thirteenth century but didn't have any systemic qualities. Financial promises lacked uniformity, and a formal system of credits didn't yet exist. A stable florin was a monumental building block, but forming a monetary system was incumbent on more than just an unwaveringly consistent coin purity. It demanded a culture of promises.

CHAPTER 2

THE EMERGENCE OF LAYERED MONEY

Always and everywhere, monetary systems are hierarchical.
—PERRY MEHRLING, Professor of Economics, Boston University

IN 1202, A TRAVELING MERCHANT BY THE NAME OF LEONARDO da Pisa, popularly known as Fibonacci, published a book called *Liber abaci* (*Book of Calculation*) that enriched the field of mathematics in Europe. Fibonacci grew up in the bazaars of Algeria where he learned of ancient mathematical discoveries, and he later published a book that brought the Hindu-Arabic numeral system to Europe, laying the foundation for the extinction of the limited Roman numeral system. He detailed advancements in arithmetic that were foreign to Europeans at the time, as well as accounting techniques that mirror methods used by merchants from India and universities from Islamic Spain.[5] These accounting techniques were the foundation of what we consider *double-entry accounting* today, the ubiquitous system of assets, liabilities, equity, and

---

5   *Gleeson-White*

profits. *Liber abaci*'s legacy would be felt right away in Italy as Fibonacci's ideas spawned a new type of merchant class, one with its power derived not from a commodity or a service but from a balance sheet: the banker.

Predating Fibonacci's book of mathematical discoveries was a monetary instrument called the *bill of exchange*. Bills were a way to send money from one place to another and simultaneously convert it to the recipient's desired currency. They were letters written by bankers promising payment. The bills weren't always paid for up front and therefore were a form of lending and an extension of credit by the issuer, making bills of exchange the world's first widely-used credit instrument. Their origin is difficult for historians to pinpoint, but we know they existed in the Arab world centuries before they arrived in Europe. By the twelfth century, bills became commonplace in northern Italy. By the fourteenth century, bill of exchange issuers denominated at least one side of practically every bill transaction in gold florin. With the florin involved in all major continental transactions, a monetary system started to emerge around this denomination. Even though hundreds of coins were circulating throughout Europe, everybody accounted in florin. It was the international business balance sheet denomination of choice and the world's first *world reserve currency*. Between the florin and bills of exchange, alongside Fibonacci's crucial innovations, a two-layered money system was starting to emerge.

In the fifteenth century, the international monetary system was finally breaking free from its (precious) metallic chains. Mathematician Luca Pacioli accelerated this process.

Pacioli taught mathematics to Leonardo da Vinci and composed a book with him called *Divina proportione* (*Divine proportions*) about architectural mathematics, but this was not Pacioli's claim to fame. Before *Divina proportione*, he published *Summa de arithmetica, geometria, proportioni et proportionalita* (*Summary of arithmetic, geometry, proportions and proportionality*) in 1494 which gave Pacioli the nickname "the father of accounting and bookkeeping." Accounting was actually only one of the teachings from his masterful summation of arithmetic, algebra, geometry, trade, and bills of exchange, but it laid the groundwork for the modern balance sheet. He formalized into scripture what had become the "Venetian Way" of double-entry accounting, a system which is still utilized by every major business entity around the world today. Within the double-entry accounting system were the secrets of how bankers could create money not by minting a coin, but from their balance sheet. Ever since *Summa*, our financial world is viewed through the lens of balance sheets, but this book aims to reframe it with layers.

The Hierarchy of Money

Let's begin to formally define *layered money*. Keeping in mind the example of a gold coin and a gold certificate from the Preface, let's take a look at an example from Renaissance Florence and the famous Medici banking dynasty. We begin this layered approach by thinking about the difference between a gold coin and a piece of paper that says, "The Medici banking family will pay one gold coin to the bearer on demand." The gold coin is a first-layer money and the form of final settlement. The piece of paper only exists because of the gold it represents; it's a second-layer money, created as a liability on somebody's balance sheet. All second-layer monies are IOUs (I-owe-you) or promises to pay first-layer money. They all have something called *counterparty risk*, or the risk that comes with holding a promise made by a counterpart. Counterparty risk is an essential concept in the monetary science, especially because all forms of money in today's financial system have some degree of it. Trust in counterparties is required for our financial system to operate, or else we'd all still be using gold and silver coins for every single transaction. Layers of money came to exist because people trusted forms of money that carried counterparty risk of the issuer. They are a way to show how monetary instruments are related to each other based on a relationship between balance sheets of financial institutions. Take a look at Figures 3 and 4, which closely mirror the Preface's example of layered money.

The layers become a way to think about money's natural hierarchy whereupon monetary instruments are ranked in order of superiority from top to bottom, instead of placed next to each other on accounting tables.[6] Each layer represents a side of somebody's balance sheet, and therefore we must also identify the actors that exist in between layers of money. In Figure 4, the Medici Banking Family is the actor

---

6 *The terms "hierarchy of money," "hierarchy of balance sheets," and "disciplinary constraint" come from Perry Mehrling's 2012 paper "The Inherent Hierarchy of Money" in which he outlines this naturally occurring hierarchy in monetary systems. His paper is foundational to the framework of this book.*

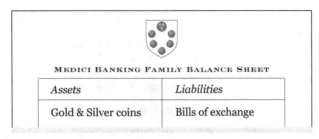

MEDICI BANKING FAMILY BALANCE SHEET	
Assets	*Liabilities*
Gold & Silver coins	Bills of exchange

Figure 3

GOLD
&
SILVER COINS

MEDICI BANKING
FAMILY

BILLS OF EXCHANGE

Figure 4

between the first and second layers. It issues second-layer money—bills of exchange, which are promises to pay first layer money—gold and silver coins. Key word: *promises*, with the risk of being broken.

Bills carried default risk by the issuer because they were a form of deferred settlement. *Default risk* is the risk that the actor between money layers cannot or will not fulfill on the promise to pay. Any bill issuer can default, leaving the holder of second-layer money with a worthless piece of paper. Despite the default risk, bills served as an instrument of monetary exchange and an accelerant to the velocity of money. Bills also greatly increased the elasticity of money; coins cannot be fashioned out of thin air, but bills could. Rubber bands are elastic: they can expand when stretched. Money can also be elastic: it can be expanded but only when it doesn't have to be fully reserved with gold coins in a vault. To merchants and their bankers, elasticity trounced default risk, and bills became the preferred monetary instrument to coins. Those willing to accept bills and other forms of deferred settlement demonstrate to us that money is fundamentally hierarchical. If a merchant demanded gold payment upfront for the delivery of goods, it was his right to do so. But if another merchant accepted a bill that represented a promise to pay gold later, his willingness to defer final settlement is proof alone that the layers of money are not a construct of bankers but immanent in the human tendency to keep tabs with each other. We began to see a system in which different layers of money served in different capacities. First-layer money emerged as a better way to store value over longer periods of time, and second-layer money emerged as a better way to transact because it was more flexible to use than coinage.

Disciplinary Constraint

The most important characteristic of the first layer of money is the disciplinary constraint it applies to layers underneath it. Here's an example. Goldsmiths in fifteenth century England weren't meager craftsmen. They also fulfilled the role of banker because of their ability to securely store precious metals better than anybody else. Let's say that an English goldsmith issues a piece of paper called a deposit for each gold coin he agrees to store. If all deposit holders suddenly ask for their gold coins back, he will easily satisfy the redemption requests because his deposits are fully reserved, meaning there is a one-to-one relationship between gold coins and gold deposits.

Let's take this opportunity to introduce the word *cash*. Monetary instruments like the gold deposits issued by trusted and reputable goldsmiths often functioned as cash. Cash is defined by anything we use as a form of money that others accept at face value, even if it's a bare piece of paper with counterparty risk and no guarantee of final payment. For something to work as cash, people have to trust the issuer, or whoever has made the promise to pay.

Back to the goldsmith. Let's say his deposits gain credibility and start circulating as cash because people trust that they are redeemable for gold. He gets greedy and decides to capitalize on his newfound trustworthiness. He issues gold deposits to himself without properly reserving the corresponding gold in his vault and spends these deposits as cash into circulation. The goldsmith will then default if ever faced with a full redemption request. This type of activity is called *fractional reserve banking*, as opposed to *full reserve banking* when all deposits have corresponding gold in a vault. Gold exists as the goldsmith's disciplinary constraint, serving as motivation not to abuse the power of money creation that comes with the public's confidence in his deposits as a form of cash. Second-layer money is therefore inherently unstable, as the power to create it will always be subject to human abuse, similar to our example of the English goldsmith who abused the public's confidence in his creditworthiness.

The hierarchy of money is dynamic, meaning that it's a set of relationships in constant flux. When credit is expanding, the money pyramid expands as the second layer grows in size. When confidence runs high, a gold coin and a gold deposit have almost no observable difference. People freely accept gold certificates as money because they trust the issuer's ability to satisfy redemption. Certificates result in convenience, as final settlement of coin and bullion can be arduous, cumbersome, and potentially dangerous. This reverses when the money pyramid enters contraction and the objective difference between money and money-like instruments is suddenly pronounced. Instruments that previously had a high degree of perceived trust are no longer desired, and their owners dump them for instruments higher in the hierarchy, such as gold coins. Contractions can result in redemption requests, called *bank runs*, and eventually financial crises. These crises can be more easily thought of as attempts to climb the pyramid of money, as holders of lower-layer money scramble to secure a superior, higher-layer form of money.

The Clearance Problem

As layered money evolved to solve problems with coin-money, new problems arose. Forms of second-layer money were all different from each other. Yet, what happened during the sixteenth century in Antwerp changed this forever: a market entirely dedicated to trading second-layer money was born. Layered money increased its velocity by bringing a tremendous advancement in the safety of its transfer: funds couldn't be lost or stolen when transferred through a banking network. Fraud and insolvency notwithstanding, the enormous reduction in shipment of coins was a huge victory for international trade. Merchant bankers sent money around the continent effortlessly by using their balance sheets and professional network instead of by shipping physical gold and silver coins. The amount of outright risk a business owner took in sending physical metal during this time cannot be underestimated. Piracy was rampant, and maritime insurance apparatuses were in their infancy. Increased usage of deferred settlement increased money velocity, as final settlement could be postponed indefinitely with only the balancing of debits and credits.

A flood of new banking liabilities and second-layer money introduced the issue of *clearance*, the process of settling transactions. No clearance system for bills of exchange existed yet. Bills weren't treated as cash due to their lack of standardization. They were promises to pay gold and silver, but they weren't fungible with each other. Customized currencies and maturity dates made each bill a static instrument that in no way resembled cash; no two bills looked alike. People weren't willing to swap letters of intent with each other because the letters' terms were all incongruent. A culture of counterparty trust hadn't yet evolved.

Slowly but surely, bill of exchange maturity dates started to gain uniformity in the fifteenth century. Dates that chronologically aligned with the European merchant fair calendar were chosen because bankers followed merchants to provide them financial services. These fairs took place throughout Europe—from France to Flanders. Merchants of cloth and silk, pepper and spices, and coins and bills gathered together seasonally to trade. The fairs were the perfect opportunity for merchant bankers from all around Europe to come and cancel out tabs with each other, or clear (as in clearance) offsetting debits and credits. The fairs' seasonal patterns, however, limited bill of exchange clearance to about four sessions per annum. That meant the second layer of money traded approximately four times per year, an objectively infrequent rate of turnover.

In the end, the second layer of money lacked *liquidity*: it couldn't easily and readily be rendered for cash. During this interval, cash and coins were synonymous, meaning that the only form of money considered to function as cash were precious metal coins themselves. Bills of exchange didn't readily convert to precious metal unless presented to the appropriate underwriters upon their maturity date. A market where bills could change hands at prices determined by buyers and sellers on location didn't exist. This would all change when the market for second-layer money left a life of quarterly clearance at traveling fairs for its first year-round home in Antwerp.

A Continuous Fair

The creation of the Antwerp Bourse in 1531 revolutionized money because it birthed the money market. At the time, the *money market* described the market for second-layer monetary instruments such as bills of exchange, gold deposits, and other promises to pay precious metal. The word *bourse* came from nearby Bruges, which previously served as the hub of northern European commerce before losing its crown when English cloth merchants decided to center their trade in Antwerp in 1421. The Bruges Bourse was a quiet meeting place for financial clearance, but the Antwerp Bourse was a place for boisterous traders and became the world's first modern financial exchange. Bourse went on to become synonymous with financial exchanges around the world; the word for "stock exchange" is *bourse* in French and *börse* in German.

Financial exchanges, like the original Antwerp Bourse, are places of trade where *price discovery* happens. Price discovery is exactly what it sounds like: the process by which an asset discovers its price by being bought and sold in a market. The price of an asset emerges, or is discovered, when observing transactions between buyers and sellers. If trade is allowed to freely occur, the price of anything can be discovered. Antwerp prided itself in its regulation-free environment, wherein the trade between first-layer coins and second-layer bills, and between bills themselves, didn't require licenses and wasn't subject to taxes. It was a haven for merchants from every country across Europe and was considered the center of the global economy during the sixteenth century. Merchants from Portugal, Spain, England, and Germany descended upon the hustling and bustling international trade hub. Antwerp's spring and autumn fairs featured English cloth, East Indian pepper peddled by the Portuguese, American silver peddled by the Spanish, and other German, Italian, and French trades. All this trade attracted merchant bankers and a litany of second-layer money issuance. When the Antwerp Bourse opened, it was known as the "Continuous Fair," depicting the evolution of financial clearance from seasonal to real-time.

Within the halls of the Antwerp Bourse the money market was born, a market that transitioned our understanding of cash from metal to paper. Bankers accomplished this by formalizing two major innovations in the evolution of layered money: discounting and note issuance. Bankers in the new Bourse didn't walk around juggling hundreds of coin-currencies all day. Coins were a detriment to money velocity, and only a combination of deferred settlement, accounting, and paper had the potential to bolster it. Initially, money market trading in the Antwerp Bourse occurred almost exclusively in bills of exchange. Money market traders gave bills of exchange liquidity, something they never had previously. This drastically increased money velocity. Before the opening of the Bourse, second-layer money was issued in quarterly increments and designed to bridge debts until the next fair. But in Antwerp, second-layer money began to develop cash-like characteristics.

The Time Value of Money

The merchant bankers of Antwerp quickly saw how using money layers, and creatively at that, could improve money as a technology for human progress. What exactly was their secret? The answer lies in one of the foundational concepts of modern finance: discounting. Let's walk through a basic example of discounting in order to illustrate the time value of money and see precisely what the bankers in Antwerp added to our monetary system.

You purchase a bill from a banker today for $98 that can be exchanged for $100 in a month. You do this because the $2 that you accrue during the month is worth the time you have to wait. This is commonly called the *time value of money* because the time you wait has value associated with it: you're paid to wait. Before the dawn of the money market in sixteenth century Antwerp, you were forced to wait a month before presenting the bill to collect your cash. In the interim, you have a piece of paper with a principal amount and a maturity date. Even though it has a maturity date in the future, this piece of paper still has value associated with it. If, after two weeks, you require liquidity from this bill and must convert it to cash, where do you go? You need a banker willing to purchase the bill for cash before it matures. The banker would split the difference between your purchase price ($98) and the face value ($100) and pay you $99. This process of a banker buying the bill at a price of $99, which is "discounted" from the $100 *par value* upon maturity, is called *discounting*. You walk away with cash today, and the banker will collect $100 at the end of the month. This type of discounting by money market traders in Antwerp brought alive the time value of money on a daily basis. Paper money finally had a price for the world to see. In fact, the birth of the financial press occurred in Antwerp during this period, not due to stock or government bond markets, but to detail daily price changes of commodities traded by merchants and second-layer money traded by bankers.[7]

---

7 *McCusker*

The last piece of the puzzle to Antwerp's success in launching the modern-day money market was the invention of promissory notes. Promissory notes brought full circle the money market's transition from a haphazard and quarterly smorgasbord to a continuous state. At the Bourse, in order to settle any outstanding balances at the end of the day, bankers issued yet another form of credit, a new second-layer money called *promissory notes* or *notes*. These notes were promises to pay the bearer, meaning that whoever held the piece of paper was due the promise. These instruments were the direct predecessors to what we consider paper cash today, currency notes. They were groundbreaking in their lack of specificity; previous versions of second-layer money always had people's names on them. Notes, like cash today, were completely free of this construct. They were used as a settlement tool but evolved into their innate role as cash and became extremely useful as mediums of exchange. Figure 5 shows the layers of money in Antwerp during the sixteenth century.

In Antwerp, the interest rate arbitrageur had arrived. *Arbitrage* is when you buy apples for $1 in one town because you know you can sell them in the next town over for $2. The art of arbitrage is as old as business itself, and medieval money changers that converted one coin into another were themselves engaged in a form of it. But arbitrage opportunities never existed in second-layer money until the Antwerp Bourse. As dealers discounted and traded bills and notes year-round in the Bourse, paper money found liquidity on any occasion, slowly moving the international monetary system away from an over-dependence on metal. The second

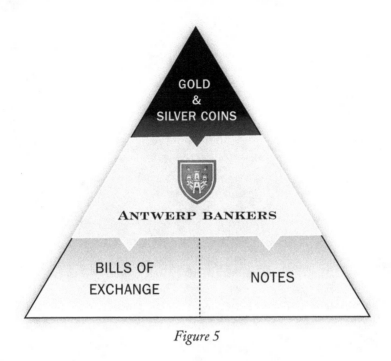

Figure 5

layer of money itself became an asset class with prices quoted by the world's first financial newspapers. The way to compare all second-layer instruments was not in terms of their individual prices but based on the interest rate one could earn from holding that paper. Interest rates were a complementary way to express the price of money, and one that allowed traders to exploit differences in the value of paper. Every piece of paper in the Bourse had an interest rate, presenting arbitrage opportunities for bankers. This modernization in liquidity ultimately shifted the primary perception of money from metal to paper. Precious metal couldn't fulfill the multitude of properties commanded from a monetary system. Accounting, paper, and a network of bankers could.

CHAPTER 3

CENTRAL BANKING

AFTER A SECOND LAYER OF MONEY EMERGED, GOVERN-ments moved to take control of the pivotal position between the first and second layers. In the seventeenth and eighteenth centuries, the Bank of Amsterdam and Bank of England inserted themselves into the money pyramid, giving their governments unprecedented power over the peoples' monetary affairs. By mandating the use of their own second-layer monies, governments and their new central bank charters removed the ability for people to have freedom of currency denomination. Governments and currencies are inextricably linked today because governments established a monopoly on second-layer money and used it to their own benefit, starting with the Bank of Amsterdam in 1609. When examining these two central banks that invented practically every aspect of what we today think of as central banking, it is essential to consider to what degree their monetary innovations served only to advance the agenda of their governments. These banks also gave us a look at what it meant to issue what the rest of the world considered to be its reserve currency. Central banks, world reserve currencies, and the arrival of third-layer money will be explored further in this chapter.

Instant Settlement

The Bank of Amsterdam (BoA) was only created thanks to the world's first joint-stock company, the Dutch East India Company (*Vereenigde Oostindische Compagnie*, or VOC). The VOC's tale begins in 1585 when the Dutch swiftly ended Antwerp's position as the center of international trade by closing off the Scheldt River and blocking access to the sea. The blockade occurred amidst the Dutch Revolt, an eighty-year struggle for Dutch freedom from the Spanish monarchy. Politically motivated, the Dutch Revolt is credited with inspiring a shift away from monarchy toward more representative forms of government in England, France, and the United States of America. The revolt resulted in the formation of the United Provinces of the Netherlands, commonly called the Dutch Republic. The founding of this new republic preceded a financial centralization that changed the face of money and business forever. The next century of the money market and all of finance concentrated in Amsterdam.

At the turn of the seventeenth century, Dutch traders were commissioning ships to the Indonesian island of Java in order to buy spices and sell them back in Europe at handsome profits. Profits attracted additional entrepreneurs, and soon a collective of international merchants started to identify with each other. Subsequent pursuits of cinnamon and ginger led to deeper profits, and soon these merchants realized their efforts could greatly multiply by joining forces and attracting capital as a unified body. The result was the first ever joint-stock company formed in 1602, the VOC. We take it for granted today, but the VOC was the first example of equity investors providing capital in exchange for a share of ownership in the form of a paper certificate. The Dutch government gave the VOC a monopoly on trade in Asia as well as the authority to hire troops and wage war on its mission to extract profit from foreign trade. The company's ability to pool capital gave it leverage to compound on its trading success. Shares in the VOC were extremely sought-after assets. As the shares increased in value, original investors wanted to realize gains by selling them for cash to new investors, and that is how the first stock market was born. The Amsterdam Bourse, named after its predecessor in Antwerp, was founded shortly after the first signs of a market for VOC shares. It was created by the VOC itself in order to facilitate the exchange of its shares on a secondary market, and with it came the ability to surveil all trading activity. Creating the Bourse allowed the VOC to observe, under its own roof, the trafficking of its shares.

The inception of the stock market led to an enormous increase in financial transactions, which demanded a settlement mechanism superior to anything that then existed. As general interest in VOC shares increased, trading increased. All share sales were simultaneous purchases of money, but what money would shareholders accept in return? They would demand cash, but accepting a bag full of random gold and silver coins wouldn't be conducive to a smoothly functioning exchange. Up to a thousand different types of coinage circulated in the new international trade hub of Amsterdam, a monetary situation too cumbersome for a city with the world's first stock market. A monetary instrument was desperately desired for payment and settlement for all these trading transactions. In 1609, the Bank of Amsterdam, or *Wisselbank*, was founded as an organic progression of financial institutions following the rise of the Amsterdam Bourse; the circulation of VOC shares necessitated an advancement in the settlement of money. Using the unit of account *guilder*, also called the Dutch florin, the Bank of Amsterdam launched a platform for free and instant settlement for all its depositors. The newly formed Dutch Republic needed its own second-layer money to support its ragingly successful colonial venture.

The BoA's first order of business was to outlaw cashiers and their notes and mandate all gold and silver coins throughout the city be deposited at the bank. Cashiers, until their activities were made illegal, were the money changers of Amsterdam. They held custody of gold and silver coins and issued paper claims against it. Cashiers were the principal actors between first- and second-layer money in Amsterdam, so in order for the BoA to attract capital, it had to do so by decree. All cashiers were forced to surrender precious metal to the Bank of Amsterdam and were issued BoA deposits in return. Cashiers were allowed to reopen business years after their ban but were only allowed to have possession of coins for a single day before being required to deposit them at the Bank of Amsterdam. The BoA was able to successfully monopolize the issuance of second-layer money by eliminating public access to first-layer money.

The BoA's deposits became a preferred money throughout Europe, especially due to Amsterdam's status as the international hub of commerce. The VOC's commodity conquests in Asia and the subsequent popularity of its groundbreaking joint-stock corporate structure unleashed a flood of capital into the city. This enabled the first true innovation of the Bank of Amsterdam: its ability to effect instant transfers among its depositors. For transactions small and large, transfers between BoA depositors became thoroughly frictionless. In order to increase the likelihood of use, the BoA didn't charge a fee for internal transfers. Transfers also did not require any exchange of coins or paper. They were solely Bank of Amsterdam accounting ledger adjustments. This all meant that with a growing number of denomination subscribers from within and outside of the Netherlands, money transfers became unimaginably easy when compared to using coins or even paper. Due to the innovation of instant settlement on the second layer of money, the Bank of Amsterdam was the first central bank, because by law the bank was central to all money dealings. The task of clearance, or settling transfers between depositors, was the foundation of central banking. The Bank of Amsterdam was a regulatory response to stock trading and a way for the government to monitor every single transaction taking place amongst its depositors. It had absolute financial surveillance over the economy because it centrally routed all of its transactions and gained a purview into the financial relationships between its patrons.[8]

8   Padgett

Demand for the BoA's denomination grew from around Europe while Amsterdam elevated its position as the continent's axis of capital. The guilder was considered the world reserve currency during the seventeenth century because merchants and businesses from all over Europe held it in reserve due to uncompromising trust in its issuer. Its status as world reserve currency lasted well into the eighteenth century.

Privileged Lending

On the Bank of Amsterdam's agenda was more than just a subtle advance in financial settlement. A closer examination suggests that the VOC positioned itself at the top of the money pyramid in order to extract power and resources. Shortly after its founding, the Bank of Amsterdam lent money to the VOC and classified the loans as assets on its balance sheet, a standard double-entry accounting practice. The BoA credited the VOC with deposits, essentially creating money and issuing it to a borrower of privilege. These loans landed right alongside gold and silver coins on the first layer of money. The VOC's creditworthiness existed on par to precious metal itself. The money created on the second layer was fractionally reserved because its corresponding first-layer asset was a loan to the VOC instead of precious metal deposited at the Bank of Amsterdam. In Figure 6, take a look at the money pyramid under the influence of the Bank of Amsterdam, portraying loans to the VOC on the first layer of money. This was a critical moment for the evolution of layered money; for the first time ever, precious metals weren't alone atop the money pyramid.

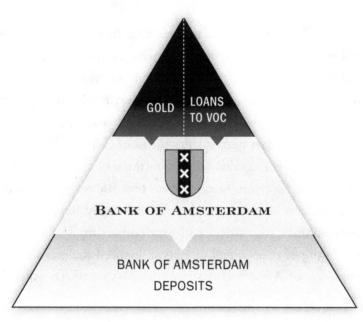

GOLD : LOANS TO VOC

BANK OF AMSTERDAM

BANK OF AMSTERDAM DEPOSITS

Figure 6

With a monopolization of the second layer, the BoA eventually eliminated the ability to withdraw precious metal altogether yet managed to maintain the public's trust in its second-layer money. The significance of this cannot be understated. By suspending convertibility to first-layer money, the Bank of Amsterdam proved that precious metal wasn't necessarily required to operate a monetary and financial system. It depended on its own disciplinary constraint to stay sufficiently reserved, and more importantly it depended on the peoples' trust in that discipline. People of Europe did trust that the Bank of Amsterdam was properly reserved and didn't issue deposits in egregious excess of its holdings of precious metal, and that trust underpinned demand for BoA deposits as money.

The Bank of Amsterdam was able to suspend convertibility by inventing another hallmark of modern-day central banking called *open market operations*, market activities by the BoA to ensure a consistent and liquid market for its deposits. By maintaining a healthy market between its deposits and other high-quality forms of cash, the BoA was able to support the value of its liabilities without ever having to surrender precious metal. This potent and unprecedented combination of instant settlement, privileged lending, and convertibility suspension had astronomic implications for the future of finance and directly influenced the creation of the Bank of Amsterdam's successor as issuer of the world's reserve currency, the Bank of England.

Bank of England

Another revolt against an unfavored monarchy preceded the Bank of England's creation. The Glorious Revolution of 1688 replaced the Catholic monarch James II with his Protestant daughter Mary and her Dutch husband, William of Orange. Although not a full transition from monarchy to republic like in the Netherlands, the Glorious Revolution in England significantly shifted power away from the monarchy toward Parliament. English jealously of and admiration for Dutch representative government and financial prowess led to a comprehensive overhaul, modernization, and centralization of the English financial system.

Nothing about the money market was centralized in England in those days. Goldsmiths fulfilled all the major roles of banking and mirrored a lot of the activity of Antwerp's first money market traders. English goldsmiths issued deposits, circulated notes, and discounted bills. The need to finance a war eventually drove the English crown to replace this decentralized system by capturing the role of sole actor between the first and second layer of money.

The English navy had freshly suffered a crushing defeat at the hands of the French and in its effort to rebuild, the government borrowed money by issuing debt. In 1694, the Bank of England (BoE) was created with the express purpose to purchase these new government bonds, and the next great central bank was born. The government and BoE drew from the privileged lending precedent set by the VOC and Bank of Amsterdam and utilized the issuance of second-layer money.

The Bank of England was additionally tasked with taking custody of precious metal, issuing deposits, effecting transfers between depositors, and circulating notes as cash. Most importantly, the BoE discounted bills of exchange and increased liquidity in the London money market. Unlike Amsterdam's monopoly on second-layer money, London was more friendly to competing versions of paper money, and the BoE's willingness and ability to discount bills when liquidity was needed the most would eventually set it apart as the archetype of central banking today.

The Gold Standard

Pound sterling has been the currency denomination of England since 1158 when King Henry introduced a silver coin of 92.5% purity.[9] The currency represented a weight in sil-

---

9   *To this day, "sterling silver" refers to silver of 92.5% purity.*

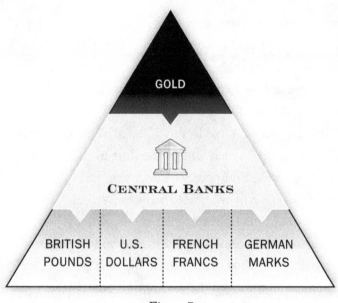

Figure 7

ver until England started minting a gold coin in 1663 called *guinea*, which was named after the part of West Africa from which the gold was mined. The guinea subjected the pound to the plaguing complications of bimetallism when both the guinea and the English silver coin called *shilling* carried official values in pounds. But shortly after the creation of the Bank of England, English mathematician and physicist Sir Isaac Newton as Master of the Mint permanently altered the course of bimetallism around the world by setting a new exchange rate between gold guineas and silver shillings in 1717. Newton studied the flow of gold and silver throughout Europe and the exchange rates set forth in other countries' bimetallic standards, specifically France, the Netherlands, and Germany. He used his findings to determine a new exchange rate between gold and silver he thought to be more representative of each metal's intrinsic value. The new exchange rate made it profitable for arbitrageurs to export silver and import gold, and before long silver stopped being used as money in England. Newton's alteration, whether premeditated or accidental, eventually brought the world under one money pyramid with only gold at the top.

Although silver was driven from usage in England shortly after Newton's alteration, it took over a century for a full *gold standard*, with which the pound became valued only in gold, to become law. England's gold standard reverberated throughout the world and eventually pulled every major country's currency into the same sphere. Figure 7 shows a layered interpretation of the international gold standard around the beginning of the twentieth century.

The Third Layer of Money

Up until now, we have extensively examined the relationship between the first and second layer of money and the financial actors that have come between them, but now we must add another layer to our framework for understanding monetary systems. Bills of exchange, from earlier examples of money pyramids, were second-layer monetary instruments that were promises to pay first-layer gold. During the Bank of England era, however, bills were promises not to pay gold but to pay pounds and therefore existed on the third layer of money. In this book we'll use the term "private sector" to describe banks, businesses, and entrepreneurs that are non-government entities. In Figure 8, we can see the private sector issues promises to pay second-layer money, placing it one layer below the Bank of England in the hierarchy of balance sheets. Liabilities of the private sector therefore exist on the third layer of money. In Figure 9, the traditional balance sheet representation is also included to orient you to the new three-layer model. Third-layer money isn't necessarily subject to *more* abuse than second-layer money, but it is in fact further away from the safety of a counterparty-free asset like gold coins. For example, if an Englishwoman feared her bank to be in a jeopardized financial position and wanted gold coins instead of third-layer bank deposits, she would require two transactions. She'd have to convert her deposits into BoE notes before converting those notes into gold. If she owned second-layer BoE notes, she would transact only once to secure the desired gold coins.

Even though the Bank of Amsterdam laid the framework for central banking, the Bank of England would eventually establish the central banking model for the world. It didn't come easily or from inception. The BoE's initial charter, issued in 1694, only guaranteed it a life of eleven years. When each charter expired, negotiations were held between the BoE and the government. In the negotiations, the government's primary concern was always to finance its spending, and the BoE's motivation was to increase its share price due to the fact that it had private shareholders motivated by profit. The BoE's shares usually appreciated sizably after charter renewals, as each one granted an extension of monetary power.

In the charter renewal of 1742, the BoE cemented its monopoly specifically over note issuance in England. The

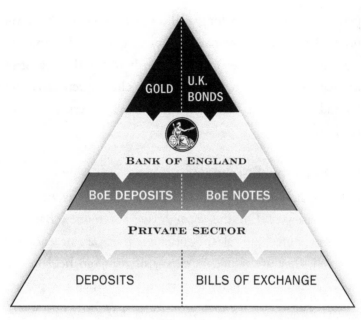

Figure 8

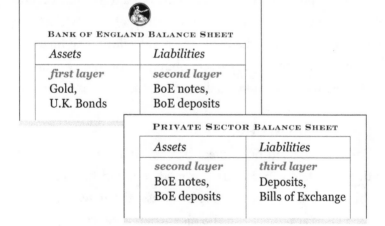

Figure 9

private sector was no longer allowed to issue second-layer notes that promised to pay the bearer gold on demand, relegating the private sector permanently to the third layer of money. The BoE faced several more charter renewals and legislation changes before finally achieving permanent status in 1844.

Elasticity and Fragility

Let's see how the elasticity of money increases as we travel lower in layers. On the second layer of money, Bank of England notes are elastic because they are fractionally reserved; they are issued in excess of the gold held in the BoE vault. This elasticity is compounded when the private sector issues deposits that promise to pay BoE notes, and those deposits themselves are only fractionally reserved by said notes. As the pyramid of money grows, lower layers in the pyramid have the most elasticity but also the most fragility as a by-product. With the backdrop of money elasticity, we can look at how the Bank of England dealt with financial panics, or the act of people scrambling up the money pyramid in order to secure more qualitatively certain forms of money.

Lender of Last Resort

Bank of England notes were demanded as cash because of their ascribed convertibility to gold coin and the creditworthiness of the sovereign. Nevertheless, the notes were still second-layer money, and the distinction between BoE notes and gold became accentuated during a particular financial crisis. The Panic of 1796, triggered by the bursting of a land bubble across the Atlantic in the newly formed United States of America, resulted in a wave of British defaults and eventually a run on the Bank of England's gold deposits. This rush out of second-layer money into first-layer gold coins would have utterly depleted the Bank of England of its gold if not for the Bank Restriction Act of 1797. The act suspended gold convertibility for all BoE notes, a suspension which lasted for over two decades. Financial panics like this one were guaranteed in a money pyramid constructed with elasticity and in a fractionally reserved manner. But the Bank of England swatted away gold's attempt to provide discipline and sent a strong message that its second-layer money could stand on its own. The fact that the BoE's liabilities could stand tall without convertibility implied that in a crisis, it could use its power to create second-layer money without undermining the currency denomination or risk losing its precious metal holdings.

The Bank of England had a way to protect its possession of gold, but it also needed a way to face crises starting in the third layer of money, for example if private sector bills of exchange suddenly lost liquidity in the money market. The BoE was willing and able to provide liquidity to the bill market by actively discounting paper that otherwise would struggle to find a price floor in crisis. In any such panic, it had to act as the ultimate backstop in an elastic system if the currency denomination were to survive.

In 1873, famed British writer and founder of the *Economist* magazine Walter Bagehot wrote a seminal book called *Lombard Street: A Description of the Money Market* that demystified how the bill market worked, and how the Bank of England should be operated in order to ensure it assuages crises. Bagehot's book is primarily cited for nominating central banks as the "lender of last resort" within a financial system. His solution was for the Bank of England to lend cash freely against creditworthy bills at punitive yet reasonable interest rates:

> *In a panic, the holders of the ultimate Bank reserve should lend to all that bring good securities quickly, freely, and readily.*

Financial crises during the era corresponded with sudden surges in the demand for cash, whereupon those either issuing or holding third-layer money required liquidity in the form of second-layer Bank of England notes. When the demand for cash swelled, Bagehot explained that second-layer money must be created by the central bank in order to satisfy that demand. It should flex its power of elasticity while still maintaining discipline in order not to encourage *moral hazard*, which occurs when a financial institution takes on excessive risk because it anticipates being rescued by the government or central bank if its financial position sours. The BoE would provide liquidity by discounting bills they deemed to be temporarily in need of support, not bills that were destined for default regardless of the financial climate. If elasticity wasn't flexed when needed, a cascade of defaults could ripple through the third layer of money. He concluded that the central bank must ultimately create second-layer money in abundance when the system needs it most, underpinning the modus operandi of central banking ever since. The power to create money came with the responsibility, when necessary, to do whatever it took to preserve the currency denomination. The pound sterling spent the nineteenth century as the world reserve currency as other nations procured it as a savings vehicle due to the British Empire's stature and stability. As the Empire expanded to cover half the Earth's surface, the Bank of England faced the enormous challenge of maintaining a domestic denomination used by participants around the world. Pound sterling wouldn't be the last currency to suffer from this conundrum. Across the Atlantic, the next world reserve currency was waiting in the wings.

CHAPTER 4

FEDERAL RESERVE SYSTEM

Gold is money. Everything else is credit.
—J.P. MORGAN to United States Congress in 1912

A T THE TURN OF THE TWENTIETH CENTURY, THE POUND remained the world's reserve currency but was losing ground to the United States dollar. During the Industrial Revolution, corporate barons Cornelius Vanderbilt, John D. Rockefeller, Andrew Carnegie, J.P. Morgan, and Henry Ford built companies that attracted demand for American currency. The world needed dollars in order to purchase the goods, services, and shares of these new elite corporate institutions. During this span, the United States did not have a central bank. But when an enormous earthquake in San Francisco induced a financial crisis in 1907, the United States would shortly thereafter take a page from Walter Bagehot's book and install a lender of last resort at the center of its financial system. The Federal Reserve System, the new American central banking apparatus, inherited a currency already on its way to world reserve status in 1914. It formalized a three-layered monetary system, with sanctioned private sector banks permitted to create third-layer monetary instruments on their balance sheets. Today, the Federal Reserve remains atop the hierarchy of money as the dollar still holds the crown of world reserve currency even though its position has become fragile. Understanding the dollar's complex dichotomy of dominance and fragility can be more easily explained with our layered terminology, a story that plays out over the next three chapters. In this chapter, we'll break down the Federal Reserve's three-layered dollar pyramid. Next, we'll see how the Federal Reserve and United States government decisively removed gold from the first layer of money. And finally, we'll look at how the international monetary system fell into disrepair starting in 2007, and why consequently the cry gets louder every year for a global currency reboot.

Early American Money

Throughout the New World colonies, money's form varied distinctly between regions. Coins weren't numerous in the early days because colonial mints didn't exist yet and European coins weren't plentiful enough to be used by everybody as currency. This drove people to use more local forms of money. In New York, sea-shell beads called wampum, used as money by many Native American tribes, circulated as legal tender during the seventeenth century. In Virginia, tobacco became a first-layer monetary asset and the basis of its own money pyramid due to the global popularity of the crop. The *pound-of-tobacco* unit became an accounting standard, and notes promising the delivery of pounds of tobacco were issued by Virginia as second-layer money that circulated among the public as cash. Shells and tobacco sufficed as regional money because they each demonstrated some, but not all, of the monetary characteristics of coinage. Neither was perfect, but they each successfully served as money for many decades. Both were divisible, difficult to conjure up, relatively fungible, and modestly durable. Eventually, they would be replaced as mediums of exchange and units of account by a historically superior form of money: gold and silver coinage.

As time elapsed, more foreign gold and silver coins started circulating as currency throughout the colonies. The most popular coin amongst the people was the Spanish silver dollar. In 1784, Thomas Jefferson published his *Notes on the Establishment of a Money Unit, and of a Coinage for the United States*, and provided the argument for the dollar as the new American currency unit:

> *[The] Dollar is a known coin, and the most familiar of all to the minds of the people. It is already adopted from South to North; has identified our currency, and therefore happily offers itself as a Unit already introduced.*

A Monetary Mix

Sixteen years after the Declaration of Independence, the second Congress of the United States of America finally passed the Coinage Act in 1792 to establish the United States *dollar* as the country's official unit of account, defining one dollar as both 1.6 grams of gold and 24 grams of silver.

For the next 108 years, the United States experimented with a few different monetary regimes. An early adjustment to the exchange rate between gold and silver had the opposite effect of Isaac Newton's adjustment as Master of the Mint and drove gold out of usage for several decades.

Two separate central banks were created in 1791 and 1812, but each ended after its twenty-year charter. Many early Americans didn't trust central banks to administer their currency. The banks existed in antithesis to limited government ideals and led to a great deal of political vitriol, which prevented the institutions from charter renewal. Instead of central bank second-layer money, notes issued by private sector banks functioned as a very serviceable form of cash throughout the nineteenth century. These notes were secured by *United States Treasuries*, the name for U.S. government bonds. Here's an example of the official language written on a currency note secured (or backed) by U.S. Treasuries from 1902:

National Currency secured by United States Bonds deposited with the Treasurer of the United States of America

The American National Bank of San Francisco will pay to the bearer on demand Ten Dollars

In addition to private sector bank notes, U.S. government-issued gold certificates also circulated as cash. And finally, a Civil War financing tool and paper money called the *greenback*, which couldn't be redeemed for precious metal, circulated as cash during the latter part of the nineteenth century as well. Altogether, the United States had an amalgamation of second-layer monetary instruments circulating throughout the country. The demarcations between the second and third layers were difficult to define, especially without a central bank and a formal monetary system. Meanwhile, an international gold standard that began in England started to permeate the globe as other European nations established second-layer currencies bearing the promise of convertibility to gold coin, which influenced a resurgence of gold usage in the United States. The Gold Standard Act of 1900 ended some monetary ambiguity, eliminating silver from its monetary role and fixed one dollar at 1.5 grams of pure gold. The corresponding price of one troy ounce of gold stood at $20.67—where it had been since 1834.[10] The act was somewhat of a formality as the Americans had already joined the world's gold standard in practice, but it was essential for the branding of the dollar denomination. The United States was now primed for another attempt at a central bank.

Reserves

In 1906, an earthquake of 7.9 magnitude rocked San Francisco, California causing mass destruction of life and property; over 3,000 people died and most of the city was destroyed. In a roundabout way, this earthquake caused the Federal Reserve System's creation. During these years, much of San Francisco's property was insured in London. British insurers paid out an enormous portion of San Francisco's colossal insurance

---

10   *A troy ounce is about 10% heavier than a regular ounce. It has been used to measure the weight of precious metals since at least the sixteenth century. Mentions of precious metal weights in this book are made in troy ounces.*

claims as a result of the earthquake, and a flurry of capital was sent to California. In order to defend the pound-to-dollar exchange rate, the Bank of England dramatically raised interest rates by 2.5% in late 1906 in an effort to attract capital away from the dollar. It worked, and the American economy entered a contractionary period, which in turn led to a financial crisis. What ensued was an all-out scramble to ditch second- and third-layer money issued by any American financial institution whose creditworthiness came even remotely into question. As Americans climbed the money pyramid in the Panic of 1907, depositors across the nation withdrew bank deposits to seek out higher-layer forms of money, like gold coins or U.S. Treasuries. These withdrawals across the country caused regional banks to run on New York banks. As the crisis escalated, banking titan J.P. Morgan stepped in, organized a financial salvation of faltering banks, and saved the financial system. Morgan didn't have a choice: a United States central bank and lender of last resort didn't exist.

The next year, United States Senator Nelson Aldrich set up the National Monetary Commission, the job of which was to study Europe's monetary system and make recommendations on how to overhaul and modernize what had become a sloppy and disjointed dollar system without a central bank. Without a government sponsored lender of last resort and clearly defined money pyramid, the dollar's internationalization remained elusive. After years of study, published reports, and congressional testimony, Aldrich finally achieved his pursuit of a central bank when Congress passed into law the Federal Reserve System on December 23, 1913.

The word *reserve* is in the title of the institution itself, but what exactly are reserves, and how do they fit into the narrative of layered money? The word implies a safety mechanism, something to help in case of a crisis. Indeed, the Federal Reserve System (the Fed) was founded to combat financial crises, and it would do this with a second-layer money called reserves. *Fed reserves* are another way to say deposits, but these deposits were issued by the Fed only to private sector banks. *Fed notes* (or the "dollar cash" we know today), the Fed's other form of second-layer money, were available to the people. Fed notes were issued as a public good, a reliable paper currency that could be easily used as a medium of exchange. But reserves are the real tool the Fed uses to wield its monetary power. They are the monetary construct we must understand to interpret the difference between wholesale money and retail money.

Wholesale money (Fed reserves) is money that banks use, and *retail money* (Fed notes) is money that people use. Fed reserves are deposits for banks only and do not have any retail access: no individual can spontaneously open up an account at their local Federal Reserve branch and acquire them. The difference between wholesale and retail money becomes more important when discussing the future of central banking, but in the historical context, the Fed's mandate was to provide wholesale money, or money for the banking system, when the instability of credit stoked financial unrest. The name said it all; the Federal Reserve system was intended primarily to be a wholesale rescue mechanism of reserves.

The Fed

The Federal Reserve Act's full name is:

> *An act to provide for the establishment of Federal reserve banks, to furnish an elastic currency, to afford means of rediscounting commercial paper, to establish a more effective supervision of banking in the United States, and for other purposes.*

The first stated purpose, "to provide for the establishment of Federal reserve banks," immediately establishes a federally unified and accepted second-layer money, "reserves," underlying all banking activity in the United States. Reserve banks would replace the existing decentralized mix of second-layer money and end the ability for private sector banks to issue it. The Act monopolized the second layer of money in the United States under the Fed, and firmly placed all private sector money issuance on the third layer.

The second stated purpose of the Act, "to furnish an elastic currency," confirmed that the Fed would have the ability to issue money in a fractionally reserved way and allow banks within its system to do the same.

The third purpose of the Act was the Walter Bagehot provision, giving the Fed the "means of rediscounting commercial paper." *Commercial paper* refers to short-term debt issued by banks and corporations. This allowed the Fed to act as a lender of last resort for the financial system by creating second-layer reserve balances in order to purchase distressed financial assets.

The last major stated purpose of the Act was "to establish a more effective supervision of banking in the United States," in an attempt to sort through the monetary disarray of the day, establish the Fed's financial surveillance on the banking industry, and give the Fed sole power to issue bank charters that came with the ability to create third-layer money.

Finally, the Act decreed that the Fed maintain a gold-coverage ratio of at least 35% against the liabilities it issued on the second layer, meaning at least 35% of the Fed's assets must be held in gold. In actuality, gold represented 84% of the Federal Reserve's assets upon its founding, a number that would dramatically fall over time. Today, for reference, gold represents less than 1% of the Fed's assets.

Initially, the Federal Reserve did not own nor intend to own U.S. Treasuries on its balance sheet. The beginning of the first World War in 1914 swiftly ended this original intent, which became irrelevant in the face of war finance. Only two years after the launch of the Federal Reserve System in 1916, the Federal Reserve Act was amended to effectively help the United States government finance its war effort, and the Fed subsequently created ample reserves in order to purchase U.S. Treasuries.

The process of building an enormous portfolio of U.S. government debt had larger implications for the dollar pyramid. U.S. Treasuries joined gold on the first layer of money because of the Fed's new asset composition: by the end of World War I in 1918, the Fed's gold-coverage ratio fell from 84% to less than 40%, as over half the Fed's assets were now held in U.S. government bonds. It was the first indication that U.S. Treasuries would eventually replace gold altogether as the dollar pyramid's only first-layer asset.

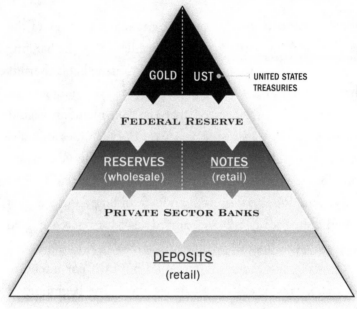

Figure 10

Figure 10 shows the three-layered dollar pyramid a few years after the Fed's creation.

CHAPTER 5

RETIRING GOLD

For both Eurodollars and liabilities of U.S. banks[,] . . .
their major source is a bookkeeper's pen.
—MILTON FRIEDMAN, Nobel Prize in Economics winner, 1976

IT ONLY TOOK HALF A CENTURY AFTER THE END OF WORLD War I for the United States to abandon its gold standard. The retirement of gold from our formal monetary system can be traced to a series of events starting with the great Wall Street crash of 1929. The 1920s, commonly referred to as the roaring twenties, was a decade defined by the first traces of consumerism: spending money as a way of life. Credit became widely available to the average American, but instead of measuring the quantity of its growth, it's more interesting to look at what type of credit was being issued. Department stores started offering credit cards to wealthy customers for the first time, oil companies began credit card loyalty programs, and banks fueled speculation in the stock market by lending up to 90% of the capital required to purchase shares. New York had become the center of international finance. Shares of companies listed on the New York Stock Exchange were flooded with demand, and capital poured into the United States. This greatly strengthened the global demand for dollars and bolstered the American currency to the world reserve currency echelon. The swarm of money creation that occurred during the roaring twenties was antagonistic toward gold's disciplinary constraint on money elasticity and conclusively revealed a societal need for the dollar's decoupling from gold. Categorically, there wasn't enough gold held by the United States government to furnish the elastic currency it had promised in its enactment. The proof of this came in the aftermath of a historic stock market crash.

When stock prices found gravity in October 1929, the Fed had to respond to a major financial crisis in earnest for the first time. With a fixed amount of gold reserves and a legally binding 35% gold-coverage ratio, the Federal Reserve was unable to create the necessary amount of second-layer money to stave off an economic depression. Several thousand banks failed in the early 1930s, wiping out billions of dollars of the American public's bank deposits. The economic depression coincided with the extremely harsh reality that third-layer money could disappear in an instant. No safety net or insurance mechanism existed to remedy such loss. The Fed did attempt to "furnish an elastic currency" and be a lender of last resort to the best of its ability, but it wasn't enough to overcome the effects of third-layer money contraction that resulted from the public's desire to flee risky deposits. The Federal Reserve was bound by a legislated minimum gold-coverage which limited the amount of credit the Fed made available to the system. Gold's disciplinary constraint received an outcry of blame for the economy's inability to recover and led to dramatic and sweeping changes to the dollar pyramid during the 1930s. These events should be seen as the major catalyst that kickstarted gold's departure from the world's monetary landscape.

No Gold for You

President Franklin Roosevelt issued Executive Order 6102 on April 5, 1933 which instructed all "gold coin, gold bullion, and certificates to be delivered to the government." The order was effectively a forced sale of gold in exchange for Federal Reserve notes (cash) by all United States citizens and outrightly eliminated the people's access to first-layer money.[11] This brazen declaration made the possession of and trafficking in first-layer money illegal and punishable by up to ten years in prison, reminiscent of the Bank of Amsterdam's mandate for all cashiers to surrender precious metal coins in exchange for BoA deposits upon its creation in 1609.

The following year, the United States passed the Gold Reserve Act of 1934, which devalued the dollar against gold by increasing the gold price from $20.67 to $35 per ounce. This immense devaluation was a surgical strike in an ongoing worldwide currency war wherein countries attempted to cheapen their currencies as much as possible relative to their trade partners. Their goal was to attract foreign demand by having the cheapest prices. The United States was merely copying what every other country was doing: giving anybody

---

11 *Executive Order 6102 was repealed in 1974 when ownership of gold was again legalized.*

with gold more buying power to purchase American goods and services. Unfortunately for the American public, the gold price increase came after the seizure, meaning the American people didn't benefit from it. The Act also legally transferred the ownership of all Federal Reserve gold to the United States Treasury and preceded the physical movement of gold bullion from New York to the United States Army's installation at Fort Knox in Kentucky.

Deposit Insurance

The Banking Act of 1935 permanently established the Federal Deposit Insurance Corporation (FDIC), institutionalizing bank deposit insurance for the average American family. In the context of layered money, FDIC insurance is a federally guaranteed insurance policy on all third-layer bank deposits. The FDIC guarantee alleviated the public's fear of third-layer money vaporizing as it did during the 4,000 bank closures in 1933 alone. In numbers, the impact of the FDIC's creation was tiny: the insured amount for each depositor was only $5,000. But from a psychological standpoint, the impact was enormous. People wouldn't flee third-layer deposits in favor of second-layer cash if they knew their deposits were insured by the federal government. Without gold as an available savings vehicle, federal deposit insurance was the government's attempt to assure citizens that their dollar savings would be protected even if housed by private sector banks with counterparty risk. Around the same time, the Federal Reserve finally secured its official monopoly over note issuance after the U.S. Treasury paid off the last bonds eligible as backing for private notes. The once ambiguous dollar pyramid suddenly started to come into focus: the monetary system existed between the second and third layers of money, and gold's constraint on lower layers had been weakened by the government's actions between 1933 and 1935. Thus, began the journey for the U.S. dollar to stand alone, independent of gold.

King Dollar

Amidst the global currency war, the dollar emerged as the cleanest dirty shirt in the laundry of global currencies. Even though the dollar devalued against gold, other countries were doing so in an even bigger way. Pound sterling abandoned a gold standard in 1931 and officially ended its reign as world reserve currency. The void was filled by the currency of the world's newest superpower: United States of America.

In 1944, world leaders gathered at a hotel in Bretton Woods, New Hampshire and formalized that all currencies besides the dollar were forms of third-layer money within the dollar pyramid. The Bretton Woods agreement would come to be known as the dollar's world reserve currency coronation. The agreement didn't impact the relationship between the first and second layers of money in any way: Federal Reserve notes still promised the bearer gold coins on demand at $35 per ounce. It did pertain, however, to the relationship between the dollar and other currencies. Currencies would have fixed exchange rates with the dollar and wouldn't themselves be redeemable for gold. Only the dollar kept a link between itself and gold. The dollar had become the axis of the world's various denominations. Governments and central

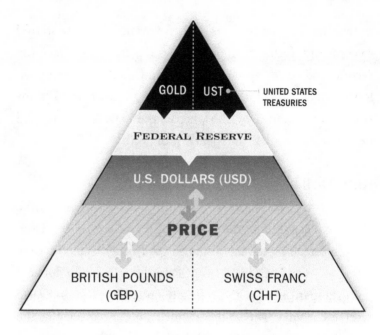

Figure 11

banks across the world were forced to shift the denomination of their reserves, securities, and balance sheets to U.S. dollars (*USD*).

The agreement brought about an important distinction in the relationship between layers of money. Foreign currencies were on the third layer of money, this time not because of the balance sheet from which they came to exist, but rather because of their price relationship to dollars. In Figure 11, we show USD on a layer above other currencies such as *GBP* (British pound sterling) and *CHF* (Swiss franc). The pound and franc are below the dollar in the layers of money because their price is measured in dollars. This means that going forward, there are two possible relationships between monetary instruments within the layered framework: balance sheet hierarchy and price hierarchy.

Destined to Fail

Unfortunately for the international monetary system, the Bretton Woods agreement was doomed. The most prescient thinker on the burden of world reserve currencies during this era was Robert Triffin, a Belgian-born economist who conducted research at the Federal Reserve and International Monetary Fund in its early years. Triffin correctly predicted the end of the Bretton Woods agreement over a decade before it collapsed. While United States citizens were banned from owning gold, foreign nations were still allowed to convert their accumulated dollar reserves to metal. Triffin predicted that these nations would eventually deplete the United States gold stock, making a fixed price of $35 per ounce of gold impossible to maintain. He warned that gold convertibility would not survive without an adjustment to the framework held in place by the Bretton Woods agreement. Most importantly, he identified that being the world reserve currency was a burden, not a blessing. Foreign countries would accumulate dollars because of its reserve status. This would strengthen the dollar and cause trade imbalances that otherwise would not exist without this extra source of world reserve currency demand. Triffin's proposed solution to the problem of one country's currency serving as the denomination of the international monetary system was political cooperation between major economic powers. In a testimony to U.S. Congress in 1959, he admitted his solution remained elusive, a dilemma that drove the demand for gold as the world's only *neutral money,* no matter how absurd the idea of it might be:

> *The logical solution of the problem . . . would have been achieved long ago if it were not for the enormous difficulties involved in . . . reaching agreement with several countries on the multiple facets of a rational system of international money and credit creation. This is, of course, the only explanation for the survival of gold itself. Nobody could have ever conceived of a more absurd waste of human resources than to dig gold in distant corners of the Earth for the sole purpose of transporting it and reburying it immediately afterward in other deep holes, especially excavated to receive it and heavily guarded to protect it. The history of human intuitions, however, has a logic of its own.*

Offshore Dollars

The story of the Eurodollar is wildly under-told. It's crucial to understanding how the entire dollar denomination was thrown into disarray during the financial crisis of 2007–2009, why the international monetary system has remained in a state of disrepair ever since, and most importantly why the world is starving for a monetary reset.

It all began in the wake of World War II after the United States dollar had unequivocally become the fulcrum of international capital and while Europe was rebuilding, financed in USD. During the Bretton Woods era, the dollar started to dominate the denomination of international commerce. Firms from around the world gravitated toward dollar denominated balance sheets. They financed their operations in dollars instead of local currency because of the dollar's deeper capital market. Demand for dollars outside of the United States skyrocketed, and banks in London, Paris, and Zurich were there to service that demand. These European banks were able to offer more attractive deposit rates than their U.S. counterparts because of regulatory differences. This steered people into European-domiciled dollar deposits. These *offshore* dollar deposits issued by banks of European origin came to be called *Eurodollars* (the word *Eurodollar* has no relation whatsoever to the *euro* currency, which didn't exist until 2001). International banks had discovered a way, without asking anybody's permission, to create dollars away from the purview of the Federal Reserve. These international banks (offshore banks) were outside the jurisdiction of the United States and therefore didn't have to adhere to any of the gold-coverage and reserve ratios set forth by the Fed and U.S. government.

Another idiosyncratic demand existed for Eurodollars: financial privacy from the United States. The 1950s were defined by the beginnings of a Cold War between capitalism and communism. Despite the political divide, the Soviets were unable to entirely avoid the almighty dollar denomination because they needed dollars to pay for all imported materials and goods required to expand their empire. The supply of dollars was both constrained and surveilled by the Federal Reserve System, so instead of relying on New York banks to hold their dollars, Soviet dollar holdings were deposited at London banks instead. By doing this, their money avoided the jurisdiction of the Federal Reserve System and United

States government. The Soviet Union communist government had a strong impetus to avoid financial surveillance and subjugation to its capitalist counterpart. The Soviets chose European bank deposits over American bank deposits even though their deposits were denominated in United States dollars.

By 1957, these new offshore dollar deposits started to trade alongside other European money market instruments in the City of London, marking the emergence of the Eurodollar market. The Eurodollar would prove not to be just another dollar-type, but rather a paradox of the international monetary system and a catalyst for its evolution. Former Federal Reserve board member and prolific author on monetary economics Charles Kindleberger described Eurodollars as a product of the natural demand for the free flow of capital around the world. In 1970, he observed that Eurodollars evolved out of necessity because the Federal Reserve System and U.S. private sector banks did not create enough second- or third-layer dollars for international users:

> *The evolution of the Eurodollar market into a world capital center, detached from the dollar in space and from Europe in currency . . . is a product not of planning by economists but of evolutionary practice. This suggests that the forces of integration in the world, of good's markets, or markets for people, and of the markets for capital are stronger than political boundaries which divide countries.*

Dollars were needed outside of the United States in order to participate in an increasingly dollarized global

Figure 12

economy. Somebody had to provide them where they were needed, even if the dollars provided only mimicked ones issued by the Federal Reserve and American banking system. By issuing Eurodollars, European banks were responding to the emergent international demand for dollars.

The dollar had become deeply entrenched as the world economy's denomination: barrels of oil were priced in dollars, trade agreements were struck in dollars, and international bank balances settled in dollars. Due to the advent of the Eurodollar, the dollar money pyramid changed. With the Fed unable to properly recognize, diagnose, or regulate the world of international banks and Eurodollars, it became unclear on which layer of money Eurodollars existed. Were they a form of third-layer money underneath Federal Reserve notes? Were they a second-layer money underneath whatever government bonds and various credit instruments the issuer owned? Or were they a new pyramid, untied to the existing dollar one? These questions wouldn't fully be answered until the great financial crisis of 2007–2009. In Figure 12, we show the Eurodollar system with a question mark at the top of the pyramid to illustrate the monetary ambiguity of international banks issuing USD.

Golden Retirement

In 1961, the first warning signs flashed that the convertibility of the dollar to gold was in grave danger. As Robert Triffin's cautions echoed louder in policymakers' ears, the United States, United Kingdom, and others came together to form the Gold Pool, whereby central banks sold precious metal into the market to keep a lid on its price at $35 per ounce. Foreign nations accumulated dollars due to its world reserve currency status and eventually began converting these dollars into gold. Redemption requests were beginning to build pressure on gold's fixed dollar price. The Gold Pool collapsed seven years later when the price officially exceeded $35 in European markets. Over the next few years, gold gracefully removed itself from the first layer of the dollar pyramid, losing its official monetary status. In 1971, the United States suspended gold convertibility for the dollar; the suspension initially was supposed to be temporary, but the dollar never returned to any linkage with the commodity. Two years later, the modern era of free-floating currencies began, officially ending the Bretton Woods agreement. Gold transitioned to the informal role of neutral money, still held today by governments and central banks around the world as first-layer, counterparty-free money.

CHAPTER 6

DOLLAR IN DISREPAIR

TODAY, OUR FINANCIAL SYSTEM IS BROKEN. IT WORKS, BUT the fractures within make it prone to ruptures. It almost collapsed in 2008 and again in 2020. The Federal Reserve has done its job as lender of last resort in each circumstance and kept the financial system alive, but everybody now understands the Fed is the world's only true source of liquidity, and without its support the system couldn't stand on its own. From a layered-money perspective, there aren't a lot of places in the dollar pyramid that don't have an explicit or implicit guarantee of liquidity backstop from the Federal Reserve today. The dollar pyramid has fractured itself in so many places since 2007, that the Federal Reserve has had no choice but to place bandages across its entire facade. This chapter tells the account of how the Federal Reserve became the world's lender of *only* resort.

A Bookkeeper's Pen

Without gold, U.S. Treasuries stood alone atop the dollar pyramid as the only first-layer money. Treasuries themselves are a form of credit, and their creditworthiness comes from the assets of the United States government and the power to collect taxes from its citizens. These government bonds became the highest-quality way to store dollars and still are today. In gold's absence, the Fed's balance sheet used U.S. Treasuries as its dominant asset, and the private sector used them as the omnipotent form of monetary collateral. For banks, ownership of these government bonds wielded the power to create yet another type of dollar called Treasury Repo dollars.

During the second World War, the United States Treasury suspended the Federal Reserve's independence with regard to monetary policy and effectively forced the Fed to finance the war effort. The Fed purchased enormous quantities of U.S. Treasuries at fixed interest rates as a result, and the United States government's quest for geopolitical dominance supplanted the Fed's politically independent monetary policy. A few years after the war ended, the Treasury-Fed Accord restored independence to the Fed, but more importantly, transitioned a vast portfolio of Treasuries into the hands of *dealer banks*, responsible for the healthy functioning of the Treasury market and *dealing* of Treasuries. These dealer banks had the power to extract liquidity from their Treasury holdings using a market for collateralized borrowing called the Treasury Repurchase (Repo) market. In a *Treasury Repo* transaction, a bank that owns a Treasury bond can pledge it as collateral and borrow money against it, just like in a pawn shop. *Treasury Repo dollar* creation occurred via the same balance sheet mechanism used for Eurodollar creation: the bookkeeper's pen. Banks could use the money they borrowed in the Treasury Repo market in interbank dollar settlement, and thus their Treasury holdings were a brand-new source of money. By 1979, the Federal Reserve concluded in a study that the explosion in Treasury Repo transactions was in fact causing an overall increase in the measurable supply of dollars and admitted not being able to make that measurement with exact precision. By 1982, the Federal Reserve fully gave up on managing the supply of dollars because they had veritably lost the ability to keep track of it; between the explosion in Eurodollars and Treasury Repo dollars, the dollar money supply had unquestionably lost all measurability. Instead, the Fed shifted to a monetary policy regime focused on managing short-term interest rates.

The Dollar's Suite of Reference Rates

Reference rates are pivotal in understanding how the dollar system broke in 2007. A reference rate is the interest rate of a credit instrument considered *risk-free* within financial academic theory. Financial theory uses the concept of a "risk-free rate" as the reference point for quantifying the risk of an investment. But credit instruments, by definition, have counterparty risk; no such thing can truly be wholly risk-free. Any borrower, no matter how mighty, can theoretically default. In reality, however, an entity like the United States Treasury has never defaulted on its debt obligations and has its own central bank to implicitly back any and all of its issuance. The Fed is the largest holder of Treasuries in the world; it is likely to purchase them ad infinitum because the purchase of

Treasuries is how the Fed creates second layer reserves into the system.[12] Also remember that in the past, the Fed was legislated into purchasing U.S. Treasuries in order to assist with war finance.

Treasuries are considered the risk-free asset in academia because financial models and valuation formulas require a baseline interest rate to reference. The entire spectrum of financial lending, from corporate debt, to residential mortgage loans, to consumer credit cards uses reference rates to set a baseline. After all, no lender would charge a family a lower interest rate to borrow than it would charge the United States government. From a layered-money perspective, instruments will always look one or two layers higher for their reference rate. Recurrently, this lands on Treasuries as the most creditworthy asset within the dollar spectrum. And in fact, it is. No other corporate, sovereign, or private entity has the track record and the implicit backing of a powerful central bank like the United States government has, landing the risk-free crown atop Treasuries. However, U.S. Treasury interest rates aren't the only reference rates in the dollar universe.

First, let's look at the differentiation between Treasuries themselves. Newly issued Treasury securities range from one month to thirty years in maturity, leading to a range of risk between Treasuries. While short-maturity Treasury

---

12 *The Fed creates reserves by purchasing U.S. Treasuries from dealer banks called Primary Dealers. Primary Dealers are an extension of the Federal Reserve's monetary policy because they are the sole recipients of second-layer money in the Fed's reserve creation process.*

Bills (T-Bills) have minimal price variability during their life, long-term Treasury Bonds have a much higher price sensitivity to changes in interest rates.[13] This sensitivity, formally called *duration*, gives long-dated U.S. Treasuries a unique and markedly different risk profile relative to their monetary cousins, T-Bills. T-Bills don't have any considerable duration and are considered the highest quality, most liquid monetary instrument one can own within the dollar denomination. The interest rate on T-Bills is therefore one of the most cited reference rates in the money market.

The Federal Reserve targets a short-term interest rate as a part of its monetary policy called the Federal Funds Rate (*Fed Funds*), an interbank lending rate for second-layer reserve deposits held at the Fed. Fed Funds is an essential reference rate because it's the Fed's desired price for short-term lending within the U.S domestic banking system.

In 1986, interest rates on Eurodollar deposits in London were formalized in a rate called LIBOR, which would express the average rate at which banks in London lent Eurodollars to each other. These dollars didn't have any connection to the Fed's second-layer reserves or third-layer dollar deposits insured by the FDIC. Nevertheless, LIBOR mirrored Fed Funds; the investing world didn't prescribe any substantial quantitative difference to the price of interbank money whether in New York or in London.

In 1998, the Fixed Income Clearing Corporation introduced an interest rate called General Collateral Financing

---

13   *T-Bills have maturities of 364 days or less, while longer-term Treasury bonds have maturities up to 30 years.*

to reflect the average collateralized lending interest rates of Treasury Repo. The concept of General Collateral (GC) started because hundreds of different Treasury securities can exist at any time, and therefore measuring the interest rate of Treasury Repo should be done by averaging interbank Treasury Repo transactions.

Interest rates for T-Bills, Fed Funds, LIBOR, and GC all mirrored each other, implying the financial system viewed these four money-types as more or less identical. The four reference rates all harmoniously trudged along in congress until August 9th, 2007, when harmony turned to discord. Before we recount that fateful day, we must start with an overview of Money Market Funds.

Money Market Funds

Most people are instinctually risk-averse. They tend to avoid conflict, or in monetary terms, they crave higher-order monies that won't default. In small amounts, FDIC insured third-layer bank deposits suffice. In large amounts, it gets more complicated. Let's bring back the example of the VOC, its shares, and the creation of the Bank of Amsterdam to illustrate the state of money today, relative to investment. In Amsterdam, shares of the VOC were speculative but rewarding to its earliest investors. When investors wanted to cash out, they required a cash-type superior to gold and silver coins stuffed into a suitcase. The Bank of Amsterdam provided that cash-type in the form of BoA deposits, which with mandated usage became a remarkably convenient way to swap between investments and cash. It was at this point that cash transitioned into a word used to describe the alternative to investments with risk. Cash now refers to a higher order of money relative to stocks and bonds, not exclusively to paper currency. In reality, no large investor can actually use paper currency with any utility: that type of cash is useless when dealing in large amounts of money. Cash today means monetary instruments that are safe relative to basically all other investments that have risk. That brings us to Money Market Funds.

Let's say you win a billion-dollar lottery. Unfortunately for you, your government exerts a 99.99% lottery tax on all winnings, leaving you with a tax bill of over $999 million dollars. The tax collector won't accept your money for a month. How do you keep the money in cash? The safest way is to purchase a T-Bill that matures on your tax due date. That way, your money is tied up in the safest possible asset until your tax bill is due. Second-layer money simply isn't an option for you: no bank has access to or the capability to store that much paper currency, and you as an individual don't have access to Fed reserves. You can keep it on deposit at your bank, but that third-layer money far exceeds the FDIC insured amount, so it carries the risk of default by the bank. If the bank is healthy, this shouldn't be a problem, but are you willing to put all your eggs in one basket and trust one single bank with a billion dollars? There is an option, however, that combines Treasuries, bank deposits, and other monetary instruments into *shares of a Money Market Fund* (*MMF shares*): a tidy cash instrument that services the world's unrelenting demand for safe money in a world of risky investments. Your best option to store your lottery winnings is by investing it in a Money Market Fund.

Money Market Funds became popular during the 1970s alongside the boom in Treasury Repo supply. MMF shares were a phenomenally desired investment product: a method to diversify away from concentrated bank risk exposure while simultaneously holding a cash-like monetary instrument. These funds had the most powerful trait possible of money; their shares held a par value relative to other high quality second- and third-layer money-types. This means that a dollar invested in MMF shares could always be redeemed for a dollar. MMFs invested in T-Bills, other U.S. Treasuries, Treasury Repo lending, commercial paper, and an array of bank liabilities.

Money Market Fund shares, depending on the exact composition of monetary instruments, became second- and third-layer money-types in their own right. Demand for MMF shares raged on as they allowed an uncomplicated way of owning a mix of monetary instruments in one security. Excess cash held by investment managers from across the world swept funds every afternoon into MMFs that in turn would purchase monetary instruments. This transformed the world's cash pool into a liquidity lifeline for multinational corporations that began to heavily rely on commercial paper funding of their operations. If, for some reason, cash holders decided to sell MMF shares for higher-layer monetary instruments, banks and corporations relying on the constant demand for their short-term obligations would face a crisis in liquidity. Therefore, the success of Money Market Funds also brought a great fragility to the financial system. Figure 13 shows what the dollar pyramid looked like as we headed for

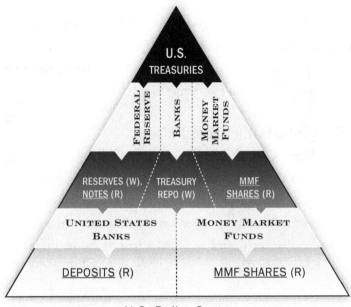

U.S. Dollar System

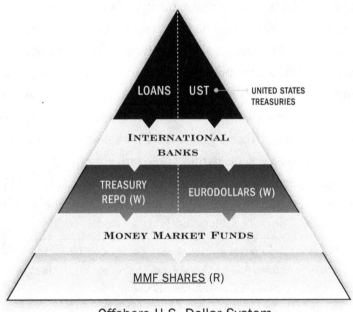

Offshore U.S. Dollar System

Figure 13

the twenty-first century and how MMF shares became the dominant form of retail money. There are two pyramids, one to represent the U.S. dollar system and another to represent the offshore U.S. dollar system.[14] [15]

When Interbank Trust Failed

Long Term Capital Management (LTCM) was a hedge fund launched in 1994 with tremendous fanfare. Its partners painted a picture of perfection with their track record. They hailed from the mighty Salomon Brothers investment bank, the Federal Reserve, and included a pair of Nobel Prize winning economists. Their art was arbitrage, much like the first bill discounters of sixteenth century Antwerp upon which the money markets were built. LTCM's competitive advantage combined interest rate arbitrage, enormous amount of leverage, and carte blanche from the world's leading investment banks. However, it all ended in ruin after the fund spectacularly failed after only four years in existence. American financial journalist Robert Lowenstein titled his book about LTCM's ultimate collapse in 1998 *When Genius Failed* in perfect summation. That a hedge fund took oversized risk and went insolvent wasn't anything new, rather a typical cycle of boom, hype, and bust. The riveting revelation from LTCM's collapse was also the smoking gun that indicated the events

---

14 *The offshore dollar system includes all banks outside of the United States and outside the jurisdiction of the Federal Reserve system, not just ones in Europe.*

15 *In Figure 13, wholesale Eurodollars include cash-instruments issued in the offshore dollar system such as Eurodollars, Certificates of Deposit, and Commercial Paper.*

of 2007 and beyond were inevitable. Shortly after the Federal Reserve bailed out LTCM's investment bank counterparties and the unwind of the infamous hedge fund itself, Federal Reserve chairman Alan Greenspan characterized the bailout as of necessity due to the prospect of a systemic collapse of the entire financial system in a testimony to U.S. Congress:

> *The issue was, in all of our judgments, that the probability [of systemic collapse] was sufficiently large to make us very uncomfortable about doing nothing . . . My own guess is that the probability was significantly below 50 percent, but still large enough to be worrisome.*

Only with the passage of time and subsequent Federal Reserve emergency actions does the gravity of Greenspan's admission begin to sink in. He confessed that the system might have collapsed had it not been for a measly $3.6 billion bailout. Why?

The answer lies in derivatives. *Derivatives* are financial contracts not considered securities. (Securities describe stocks and bonds for example, and derivatives describe stock options, futures contracts, and interest rate swaps.) Derivatives blossomed in the 1990s as a way to synthetically expose a portfolio to an array of outcomes, most commonly the fluctuation of interest rates. They were bank liabilities in a new form, one that was difficult for financial regulators or even the banking system as a whole to fully comprehend. Most illustratively though, derivatives existed as a tangled web of financial obligations within the banking system, concentrating risk in the relationships between a handful of banks in the United States and Europe. An enormous margin call from the investment bank and major LTCM counterparty Bear Stearns in September 1998 triggered a collective realization that derivatives held by the hedge fund had the power to bring down the entire house of flimsy interbank risk.

At the time of the LTCM bailout, the total market value of all the world's derivatives including interest rate swaps, credit default swaps, and foreign exchange currency swaps was $3 trillion. To compare, the total supply of U.S. Treasuries was also about $3 trillion. By 2007, the total supply of U.S. Treasuries increased to $4 trillion but the market value of derivatives outstanding increased to $11 trillion. While the $4 trillion in Treasuries stood upon a bicentennial tradition of creditworthiness, conversely, the $11 trillion unsustainably teetered on the thin and fraying wires of interbank trust.[16]

Falling into Disrepair

Despite cracks in the dollar pyramid's foundation that surfaced after the LTCM bailout, money market interest rates portrayed a sturdier facade. U.S. Treasury Bills, Fed Funds, Eurodollar LIBOR, and Treasury Repo GC rates all closely tracked each other for years. Small divergences would occur but were always characterized as the result of seasonal or idiosyncratic factors. That would all change starting on August 9, 2007. On that day, LIBOR rose by what might seem like a paltry 0.12% relative to the rest of the family of money market

---

16 *BIS data*

rates, but it was the start of something dramatic. The night before, French bank BNP Paribas was unwilling to value certain derivatives and froze all cash withdrawals for funds holding financial instruments related to risky American home borrowers. A sudden jolt of distrust electrocuted the interbank funding market in the weeks to follow. Banks were afraid to lend money to each other in any capacity because they weren't sure which banks might not open back up the next day. The era of unlimited, almost care-free interbank exposure had ended, replaced by extreme caution and nervousness. The ascent up the dollar pyramid had begun.

On December 12, 2007, the Federal Reserve was finally forced to address the gargantuan elephant in the room, which was that European interbank trust and the "bookkeeper's pen" Eurodollar funding mechanisms had broken down. A contraction in European interbank trust, expressed by a rising LIBOR, was causing the whole dollar pyramid to rattle like an earthquake. The Fed instituted foreign exchange swap lines to the European Central Bank and Swiss National Bank in order to provide liquidity to the offshore banking system, having to turn a blind eye to the practice of creating dollar liabilities outside the Fed's purview. The Fed's role as lender of last resort had expanded beyond its borders because of the complicated evolution of the international monetary system, not because its mandate all of a sudden switched from domestic to global monetary policy. This conundrum was neither escapable nor up for discussion considering that the international monetary system was unabashedly dependent upon the Federal Reserve as the lender of *only* resort.

These foreign exchange swaps created yet another type of second-layer money made available by the Federal Reserve exclusively to other select central banks.

Amidst a wave of American mortgage defaults in 2008, the intricate web of failing mortgage derivatives started causing lower layers of the dollar pyramid to crumble with dramatic and permanent consequences. When the prestigious investment bank Lehman Brothers failed on September 15, 2008, a money market fund called Reserve Primary Fund famously "broke the buck" when it posted a share price of $0.97 because it owned a fair amount of newly defaulted Lehman Brothers commercial paper. This drop of a mere three cents from par triggered an all-out financial panic that elicited unprecedented emergency actions from central banks and governments around the world. The reason for the panic wasn't necessarily the three-cent drop, but the fear that if Lehman Brothers commercial paper could fail, and Reserve Primary Fund's shares weren't worth a whole dollar, *nothing* could be trusted. All forms of bank liabilities lost liquidity, and the financial system froze. Time stood still, as nobody knew if banks would open the following day.

The Fed fulfilled its role as lender of only resort by launching a slew of consecutive rescues to stave off systemic collapse. The insurance giant American International Group (AIG) received a Fed lifeline on September 16th because it had underwritten insurance on risky mortgage securities that were suddenly defaulting. The entire Money Market Fund complex received a guarantee from the Fed on September 19th that its share prices would be supported to prevent withdrawal panic. Goldman Sachs and Morgan Stanley received their lifeline on September 22nd after being allowed to convert from investment banks into bank holding companies which gave them direct access to Fed lending. Concurrently, the Fed was increasing liquidity capacity for major central banks across the world on a daily basis. It was an all-out capitulation from the Fed to avoid systemic collapse.

Despite the Fed backstopping each and every form of cash it could, the ongoing liquidation of inferior assets and ascent up the dollar pyramid persisted. The original intent of the Federal Reserve System was to provide a second layer of money elastic enough to withstand shocks to the system exactly like this one. On November 25th, the Federal Reserve had no other choice than to flood the system with reserves by purchasing U.S. Treasuries, many of which had been newly issued in order to finance enormous deficits resulting from economic recession, tax shortfalls, and corporate bailouts. Large-scale expansion of second-layer money by the Fed was a response to contraction elsewhere in the system; it had to meet the collapse in interbank trust and liquidity with its own reliable liquidity. The Fed called it Quantitative Easing (QE), but we can refer to it as second-layer money creation.

Interbank trust only decayed in the years after the financial crisis of 2007–2009. Banks started dialing back their exposure to each other during the fourth quarter of each year to prepare for year-end regulatory snapshots. Divergences in key money market interest rate spreads—like when LIBOR split from Fed Funds and others in August 2007—occurred more often, especially around calendar events such as the end of each quarter and United States tax deadlines. Complete dislocations would occur, indicating that money needed at certain times during the year wasn't necessarily available to those who needed it most. Liquidity was haphazard, to say the least. The Fed had slashed the price of money and targeted interest rates of 0%, backstopped the unknown quality Eurodollar market, and created trillions of dollars of reserves to bolster the American banking system, but for what? When the Fed eventually tried to unwind its emergency actions years later, it was unable to raise interest rates above 2% without financial panic briefly rearing its ugly head again. The Fed quickly reversed course upon becoming reacquainted with the dollar system's fragility. A return to peaceful money markets was unattainable, as the Fed had removed price discovery from the system by disallowing so many third-layer money-types from realizing their ultimate fate.

Lender of Only Resort

Much like several of the money market dislocations of the 2010s, the initial blame for the Treasury Repo crisis in September 2019 was ascribed to the United States corporate tax deadline. The financial media's narrative was: MMF shares were sold by corporations so they could pay their tax obligations which in turn depleted the Treasury Repo lending base, but that Treasury Repo liquidity would return quickly much like in the days after other calendar events. On September 16th, the spread of General Collateral to Fed Funds increased by 0.10%, but nobody blinked an eye. Moves of this size had become quite standard in the years since the notorious day in August 2007 when LIBOR became disjointed from the rest of the money market.

The next day, however, would live in Treasury Repo infamy. By late morning, the Treasury Repo GC rate registered at an alarming 8% higher than Fed Funds, indicating that at least one bank holding U.S. Treasuries could not find a counterparty to lend money against its Treasury collateral. The Federal Reserve responded with an emergency Treasury Repo funding operation later that day, effectively backstopping the entire market for Treasury-collateralized lending. The measures were supposed to be temporary as seasonal factors were surely to blame, but it didn't play out as such. The Fed increased its commitment to a smoothly functioning Treasury Repo market by cementing its willingness to lend freely against Treasury collateral so that what happened on September 17, 2019 would never happen again. After saving the Eurodollar in December 2007, the Fed had liberated yet another dollar-type in Treasury Repo and made a trend out of institutionalizing dollar-types gone astray. The Fed continued to find new ways to create wholesale second-layer money in order to counter instability.

During the pandemic-induced global financial panic of March 2020, the Federal Reserve announced several additional lending facilities to further backstop the Treasury Repo market, Money Market Funds, and fifteen additional foreign central banks. To protect the system against foreign liquidation of U.S. Treasuries, the Fed instituted a facility to lend money in the Treasury Repo market to approved foreign entities so that these governments and central banks didn't disrupt the Treasury market if they ever needed cash: they could post their Treasuries as collateral directly at the Fed's pawn shop. Even though Treasury prices soared in the first few days of pandemic panic as unlimited demand emerged for the world's safest asset amidst collapsing prices of stocks and corporate bonds, they didn't remain impervious. U.S. Treasuries with longer maturities (ten to thirty years) suddenly lost a bid despite their typical safe-haven status because of all the chaos in the markets.[17] Members of the Fed panicked: a malfunctioning Treasury market was a recipe for disaster. What followed was a wave of U.S. Treasury purchases and reserve creation by the Fed that made the 2008–2010 Quantitative Easing programs look like a practice run. The Fed convened over the weekend and announced a new, unlimited QE program of Treasury purchases without any defined maximum in order to mollify all concerns that the Fed might let the world's most important security market experience any sustained disturbance.

Money-types around the world were losing their ability to survive independent of the Federal Reserve. While it never lost its position atop the dollar money pyramid, the Fed has with some degree of success managed to claw back power over sections previously outside of its purview, mostly due to the fact that as each money-type almost failed, the

---

17 *An arbitrage trade by large hedge funds between Treasury bonds and Treasury futures derivatives contracts has received blame for causing enormous disruptions in the Treasury market in March 2020, however the debate continues.*

Fed stepped in to save the day. The whole system has become entirely beholden to its support. Yet despite the dollar system's fragility that has been exposed over the past dozen years, the dollar is more deeply entrenched as the international monetary system's fulcrum than ever. The world is seemingly trapped inside a dollar denomination and is hankering for a monetary renaissance. Each crisis seems to be unraveling more quickly than the previous one as the system becomes dramatically more fragile.

Taking a step back, we have to understand why the Fed is creating all this second-layer money in the form of reserves, Treasury Repo lending, foreign exchange swap lending, and other bailout mechanisms. It does this because the Fed is a wholesale money safety net. Unless it flies a fleet of helicopters over American cities and unloads crates of second-layer retail money (Fed notes or cash), it does not have a way to provide money in a retail setting to individuals. The only way the Fed can provide monetary stimulus is to provide wholesale money where it is needed most within the financial system. The Federal Reserve is meant to provide reserves, and currently it possesses no political authority to issue retail monetary stimulus. This might change in the future and will be discussed in Chapter 9.

Tales of the dollar's demise are premature. While their arguments have mathematical merit given just how much money the Fed has created, they lack cohesiveness when considering the alternatives. The dollar is still the undisputed world reserve currency. Half of all international invoices are denominated in USD even though the American economy comprises only 15% of the global economy. Despite all the worthy criticisms about the Federal Reserve's seemingly infinite dollar creation, the dollar's stature as an accounting denomination, preferred method of payment for international commerce, and capital market funding currency is nothing short of dominant. Its dominance is unlikely to fade away over the next several years. U.S. Treasuries remain the only asset that has the proven market liquidity and depth required to don the title of risk-free asset. The dollar has become so ephemeral in nature that the only way to truly store dollars over time is to own a portfolio of U.S Treasuries. That is why dollars travel around on the second and third layer of money, but only U.S. Treasuries can call themselves first-layer money in the dollar pyramid. The depth and liquidity of the U.S. Treasury market doesn't preempt the decision to store capital in the dollar denomination, it's actually the only thing holding it together because of the uncertainty that stems from owning bank-issued third-layer money.

CHAPTER 7

A RENAISSANCE
OF MONEY

ORTY-SIX DAYS AFTER THE FALL OF LEHMAN BROTHERS in 2008 and directly amidst the world's collective realization of the dollar system's precarious position, a presciently timed white paper was sent to a very small online community called the Cryptography Mailing List. The paper was written for members of the cryptography discipline, not the monetary one, and therefore it didn't even register as relevant to money back then. Looking back, however, we *must* with authority insert this day, October 31, 2008 and the creation of Bitcoin into the official record of monetary evolution. The date is momentous not only because the paper proposed an alternative to our current financial infrastructure, but also because of what ensued. Bitcoin, a novel monetary instrument, is now owned by at least 1% of the world's current population, or about 100 million people.[18] Vehement criticism of Bitcoin's rise from politicians, bankers, and the financial media has

---

18 *A University of Cambridge study estimated there are 101 million unique "Total Cryptoasset Users" across 191 million accounts globally in September 2020.*

occurred alongside an exponential increase in its user base and market value. Bitcoin's arrival, growth, and staying power now warrants an honest, well-researched, and holistic view of this new monetary technology. Instead of dismissing Bitcoin as an unregulated and unbacked currency, we must instead try to understand why exactly Bitcoin has amassed such a groundswell of attention and market value. In only twelve years, it has already captured about 6% of gold's total market value despite gold's several thousand-year head start.[19]

In the realm of monetary science, Bitcoin is an alien invader. It doesn't resemble anything that came before it because it relies heavily on technological innovations of the past half-century. An area of computer science called *applied cryptography* crept up on the financial system and startled it. The invasion continues to reverberate with each passing year of Bitcoin's growth in mind share. When we look back at Bitcoin's origin through this book's layered lens, we can see that a new first-layer money had been invented and that the monetary and cryptography sciences had merged. The unification is only now, a dozen years after Bitcoin's creation, becoming accepted as a monetary discipline. Before we speculate on how it will play out, we must understand Bitcoin's origin, early history, and the evolution of its own money pyramid.

---

19 *The BTC/USD price and total market value used throughout this book were $34,000 and $630 billion, respectively, a snapshot taken on Bitcoin's twelfth birthday, January 3, 2021. Data: Coin Metrics.*

Satoshi Nakamoto and the Bitcoin White Paper

The paper published on October 31, 2008 that changed the world of money forever was written by Satoshi Nakamoto. Anonymity and mystery surround the Satoshi persona and his, her, or their writings. The creator remains unknown even now, something that strengthens Bitcoin's neutrality, as no leader exists who wields too much influence, can be coerced or blackmailed, or will try to change Bitcoin's rules. The importance of the architect's identity is now arguably irrelevant, but it still doesn't diminish the intrigue of the facelessness; Satoshi would send his last known correspondence in April 2011 and disappeared from the Internet forever.[20] The myth and legend of Satoshi will make a grippingly dramatic film one day, but the software he designed forever changed the very notion of money. The first sentence of Satoshi Nakamoto's paper "Bitcoin: A Peer-to-Peer Electronic Cash System" read:

> *A purely peer-to-peer version of electronic cash would allow online payments to be sent directly from one party to another without going through a financial institution.*

A transferable online cash without financial institutions implied coordination, but how, and by what rules? The only globally accepted and neutral money not relying on a financial institution is gold. The most fascinating component of Satoshi's design of Bitcoin was his intention for it to mimic

---

20 *This book will use "he/his" to refer to Satoshi Nakamoto for simplicity while acknowledging that Satoshi's identity remains unknown.*

gold as a first-layer, counterparty-free money. And that meant a supply that does *not* originate from a balance sheet. Satoshi's paper built upon foundational and widely accepted cryptography building blocks which legitimized his idea among some members of the Cryptography Mailing List.

Defining Bitcoin

The word "Bitcoin" officially refers to two things, (1) the *Bitcoin* software protocol and (2) the monetary unit within that software. In this book, we'll refer to the monetary unit as *BTC* in a distinction from the software itself. Bitcoin, the software *protocol*, is a set of rules. It uses a military-grade encryption algorithm called Secure Hash Algorithm 2 (SHA2), first published by the U.S. intelligence community in 2001.[21] Usage of SHA2 is considered so secure that it's actually required by law within areas of government that handle highly sensitive information. Bitcoin's design combines SHA2 with intelligent rules so elegant that it's able to embody gold's monetary properties in the digital world. Bottom line, the cryptography used by Satoshi was proven and secure. These ingenious rules built a coordination mechanism that he called a "chain of blocks," but the world would come to call it Bitcoin's blockchain.

Computer Science

Before diving into the specific technical innovations of Bitcoin's blockchain that made it a successful digital currency, we have to acknowledge that understanding Bitcoin on a technical level requires an abundance of computer science

---

21 *Bitcoin uses a specific type of SHA2 called SHA-256*

expertise. Textbooks have been written on the Bitcoin software, filled with programming-level detail on all of Bitcoin's major components including keys, addresses, wallets, transactions, and mining. In the next two chapters, we will discuss and explain these components, but for those that want a more immersive experience in the brilliant cryptography behind the Bitcoin software, start with "Mastering Bitcoin" by Andreas Antonopolous. It is written in a way that is approachable even to those who don't have a strong computer science background but are curious about the rules that make Bitcoin work. For everybody else, understand that Bitcoin's rules make it a trusted digital currency much in the same way that people trust email for digital communication. They might not know exactly how it works, but it does.

Useful Bitcoin Analogies

Let's first explore three elementary metaphors for Bitcoin: gold, land, and email.

BTC is digital gold. It's a form of money. People trust BTC because they believe it to be rare and valuable in a very similar way to how people for millennia have put their faith in gold. It has a price in hundreds of different currencies, just like gold does. And most importantly, it doesn't originate from the balance sheet of a financial institution, just like gold doesn't. Gold and BTC are both counterparty-free assets. We'll have the opportunity to draw more sweeping comparisons to gold throughout the rest of the book.

BTC is digital land. There are only 57 million square miles of land on Earth. Similarly, there will only be 21 million BTC.

Thankfully, this digital land is divisible into the tiniest of parcels.[22] Mark Twain once said "buy land, they're not making it anymore" to endorse investment in real estate, and BTC can be thought of in the same way. BTC is scarce, akin to the amount of land on Earth. We'll explore how it achieves scarcity shortly, but as more people journey from British pounds, Japanese yen, and U.S. dollars to the Bitcoin world, this digital land will only become harder to acquire at current prices. We can liken BTC's price rise to a land grab and explain its exponential increase in market value and adoption as mirroring the Internet in the 1990s. The price for a slice of the Bitcoin pie has risen steadily over the long-term because people are treating it like prime real estate. There is no single gatekeeper in the Bitcoin realm, making every human being a potential property owner. Ownership will become more expensive as its world gets more crowded; once people finally understand the renaissance of money taking place, the fear of missing out will become overwhelming.

Lastly, Bitcoin works similarly to email. You might not understand the computer science behind how it works, but the basic action of sending and receiving email is a universal practice. Email addresses can be shared with anybody, but only the password holder can access received messages. Bitcoin works in a similar way. You can share your Bitcoin address with anybody sending you money, but only with your password, called a *private key*, can you spend it. Email is a

---

22 *There are 100,000,000 sats, named after Satoshi, in 1 BTC. Sats are BTC's sub-unit (think of dollars and cents). 21,000,000 BTC = 2,100,000,000,000,000 sats.*

protocol to send and receive data; its formal name is Simple Mail Transfer Protocol (SMTP). Bitcoin is also a protocol, but to send and receive value instead of data.

Blockchain and Bitcoin Mining

What makes Bitcoin tantamount to gold, human civilization's most proven monetary asset? The answer lies in the rules of the Bitcoin protocol.

The Bitcoin blockchain most fundamentally describes a record of transactions simultaneously kept by all peers in the network. In order to properly define blocks and chains, let's first dive a little deeper into the word *peer*. In Bitcoin terms, anybody can be a peer by operating a Bitcoin *node*, which is a computing device running the Bitcoin software. Only those that operate a Bitcoin node are using it in a wholly *trustless* way, meaning they are only relying on their own software to verify the settlement of BTC transactions (trustless can be thought of as the opposite of "having counterparty risk"). They are not delegating to any bank, exchange, or software company. The magic of Bitcoin is that every single person in the world can become a peer and operate a software that allows participation in a global financial network. Most people rely on some form of provider to interact with Bitcoin however, such as smartphone applications for wallets and exchanges for trading and custody. Wallets and exchanges are like the banks of the Bitcoin industry; as people count on banks to interact with their USD or home currency, people rely on wallet companies and exchanges to interact with their BTC. But they don't have to, and that is what makes Bitcoin so powerful. Anybody with a computer and the Internet can transact globally without depending on any single company, government, or entity. Using the Bitcoin software should only be done by people with a high degree of proficiency, and therefore most will trust the private sector for that expertise.

Now we can define blocks. A *block* is a set of data that includes the details of unsettled Bitcoin transactions that people are trying to complete. These transactions can be thought of as emails that have been sent but not yet received, or existing only in cyberspace. Blocks become chained together and unsettled transactions get confirmed when a block is mined. But what exactly is mining?

Just as gold miners expend energy to dig gold out of the Earth's crust, Bitcoin *miners*, peers that compete over new supply of BTC, expend energy that award them the currency within the Bitcoin software. Bitcoin miners are awarded BTC when they find a random number; think of it as a computational lottery. In order to find that number, they perform trillions of computations every second. That makes Bitcoin mining virtually one giant random-numbers game, and only the fastest and most powerful computers can compete in a game in which computational guessing is most valued. In the early days of the Bitcoin network, BTC could be successfully mined by anybody using the average laptop. Today, highly efficient supercomputers called ASICs (application-specific integrated circuits) are required to successfully mine BTC. Technical expertise isn't necessarily warranted; electricity, ASICs, and software give anybody access to participate in the process of BTC supply introduction. Miners are financially motivated; they are awarded BTC for their services which they can keep or exchange for local currency. They help make the Bitcoin network more secure by dedicating a tidal wave of energy and computing power toward adding blocks to the chain. This tidal wave is commonly referred to as *hashpower*, with the word "hash" coming from Secure Hash Algorithm 2 (SHA2) used by the Bitcoin software for encryption. Bitcoin mining is also called performing *proof-of-work*, which was invented before Bitcoin in 2002 by cryptographer Adam Back, who holds a Ph.D. in computer science from the University of Exeter. Satoshi Nakamoto cites Back in his white paper and bases much of Bitcoin's original credibility upon using proof-of-work, a proven technology by 2008. Proof-of-work in Bitcoin is equivalent to digging for gold as stated in the Bitcoin white paper:

The steady addition of a constant amount of new coins is analogous to gold miners expending resources to add gold to circulation.

Make no mistake, this isn't just an analogy. Satoshi Nakamoto was tremendously deliberate in the design of Bitcoin; it was meant to mimic gold because gold is historically our planet's most enduring counterparty-free form of money. Finding gold isn't cheap or easy; it requires energy, as does finding BTC. Once a miner successfully mines a block and wins BTC as a result, the block becomes an update to Bitcoin's shared transaction ledger so that every peer in the network has the latest understanding of which

Bitcoin addresses are associated with exactly how much BTC. Blocks become *chained* together during this process to leave an accounting record, the Bitcoin blockchain, for all peers to witness. The term *blockchain* has grown in popularity, but *distributed ledger technology* is a simpler way to describe a network structure whereby all peers keep a ledger, or a record of transactions. For this reason, the term Distributed Ledger Technology (DLT) has been adopted by central banking research departments to describe software that mimics Bitcoin's original distributed ledger design.

How much BTC does a miner earn when successfully mining a block, and who determined the supply of BTC? The next component of Satoshi's elaborate design lies in Bitcoin's monetary policy, or the rules around the supply of BTC and how it comes into existence. Not set by human beings in the boardroom of a central bank, Bitcoin's monetary policy is an algorithm programmed by Satoshi in 2008 to specify its exact issuance schedule into eternity. The issuance rules were coherent, elegant, and just. They felt fair to the earliest participants in the network. For the first 210,000 blocks (or approximately four years) of Bitcoin's existence, 50 BTC was awarded to the successful miner of each block. For the next 210,000 blocks, the reward fell to 25 BTC per block. Each passing 210,000 blocks, the mining reward halves again. Each of these *epochs*, or periods of time to complete each phase of Bitcoin's issuance schedule (210,000 blocks or ~4 years), show how Bitcoin's monetary policy is set in stone, not up for debate in the halls and teleconferences of central banks. Bitcoin is currently in its fourth epoch with the mining reward standing at 6.25 BTC per block, which is valued at over $200,000 today. Satoshi mapped out the supply schedule all the way until the final block reward estimated to occur over a century from now in 2140. Why he chose 21 million as BTC's ultimate supply or 210,000 block epochs will probably remain an enigma, but something about the mathematical precision of it all vehemently attracted people. The exact scarcity specified at the beginning of Bitcoin's existence isn't even necessarily an impressive feat. What's impressive is that every participant in the network coalesced around it and the associated supply schedule rules to form a true consensus about Bitcoin. Its scarcity and the rules that secured it not only persisted, but they also quickly became written in stone.

The Bitcoin protocol mandates that blocks occur on average ten minutes apart, but the actual time between blocks can take seconds or hours depending on how long it takes a miner to win each proverbial BTC lottery. The algorithm that adjusts the computational lottery every two weeks to make sure blocks occur on average ten minutes apart, called the *difficulty adjustment*, was designed by Satoshi Nakamoto and has been working like clockwork for the entirety of Bitcoin's existence. No single peer has control over the entirely automated difficulty adjustment. The difficulty adjustment algorithm is considered untouchable by Bitcoin's users and software developers today because it is one of the properties of Bitcoin that makes it truly neutral and resistant to centralized control. With superior mining ASICs, a miner can win an outsized proportion of block rewards, but eventually Bitcoin immunizes itself to improvements in computer processing power by gradually diluting advantages away. Regular increases in mining difficulty function as one of Bitcoin's security mechanisms, preventing today's fastest computers from running away with block rewards and driving innovation in computer chip manufacturing. The rules surrounding the supply of Bitcoin have become tamper-proof, incorruptible, and the new gold standard for monetary scarcity. The result of Bitcoin's unique and brilliant rule set is a truly novel form of money. With razor precision and free software, one can measure exactly how rare his or her BTC collateral is at any moment.

Send and Receive

The final technical component to understand about Bitcoin is the relationship between keys and addresses and how peers send and receive BTC. *Addresses*, which are used to receive BTC, are generated from numbers called *private keys*. This effectively means that possession of BTC itself is the possession of a number. Private keys are 256-character binary strings, like this:

11011010010001000110101101010101001100110010010000011011001111010
01010101011011011100011001001001011100100100101100100010101100
01011100000111011001111010111001011111111111101101111110011011101
00011101101010000101100100100101100001110011100111001011100000
00010011110110110010101

These numbers can be stored in smartphone applications called *wallets*, on dedicated memory devices called *hard wallets*, simply written down on a piece of paper, or frankly in any way you can store a number. The private keys generate an address that is used in order to receive BTC, but the address cannot be reverse engineered to reveal the private key behind it, thanks to SHA2 encryption technology. Bitcoin addresses look something like this:

32bp4f8zjbA8Bzm3TiAq5jav3DsU4LPSQR

That's it: private keys (send) and addresses (receive). BTC can be sent around the network after it's mined without any central router to authorize or censor the transactions. Any peer in the network with Bitcoin software can send, receive, and surveil transactions, but no single peer can prevent them from happening. Note that people using a smartphone wallet do not need the full Bitcoin software in order to transact in BTC; wallets allow people to self-custody BTC private keys but rely on third-party nodes to relay transactions to the network if not used in tandem with a Bitcoin node.

A New Denomination

In the digital realm, Bitcoin's software facilitates and clears all transactions within its denomination. It functions like a central bank from the settlement perspective, only instead of central, the software is anywhere that Bitcoin nodes exist. Bitcoin's innovation created an entirely new denomination and payments infrastructure, controlled by nobody. Digital payments were already ubiquitous by 2009 with the widespread use of online credit card payments, PayPal, and other smartphone payment applications used to transact third-layer bank deposits. But until Bitcoin, nobody had figured out how to mimic cash and final settlement on the first layer of money without using a central entity. As the Internet's native currency denomination, payment system, and digital gold all rolled into one, Bitcoin became a force to be reckoned with very early into its existence. It was arguably the most important monetary breakthrough since gold coinage almost three thousand years ago: scarce, mathematically certain, free and open to use, and immune to greed.

Policy makers around the world must heed the connotation of a new monetary denomination. The United States of America in particular prides itself on its freedom of speech, and its treatment of this new monetary technology should be no different. Bitcoin is a form of speech: people should be allowed to transmit a message (send a BTC transaction) as freely as they are able to send an email. Bitcoin is a numerical software, and any attempt to ban or restrict the usage of Bitcoin by governments would be a ban or restriction on math itself. The United States judicial system has already established the precedent that the use of encryption is a requirement to protect free speech in the digital era, and the same ideas should be applied to Bitcoin in every corner of the world that prides itself on the freedom of its citizens. Here is a 1999 ruling by the United States Court of Appeals, Ninth Circuit (Bernstein v. United States), confirming that encryption, like math, is an expression of scientific ideas and therefore a form of speech:

> *Cryptographers use source code to express their scientific ideas in much the same way that mathematicians use equations or*

economists use graphs. Of course, both mathematical equations and graphs are used in other fields for many purposes, not all of which are expressive. But mathematicians and economists have adopted these modes of expression in order to facilitate the precise and rigorous expression of complex scientific ideas. Similarly, the undisputed record here makes it clear that cryptographers utilize source code in the same fashion. In light of these considerations, we conclude that encryption software, in its source code form and as employed by those in the field of cryptography, must be viewed as expressive for First Amendment purposes.

Buying Coffee with Bitcoin

The Bitcoin transaction settlement process is simultaneously consistent and highly irregular. Let's look at an example of somebody trying to use BTC to make a purchase. A woman walks into a café to buy a cup of coffee. The café accepts BTC as payment and charges 15,000 *sats* (0.00015 BTC, or approximately $5) for coffee. The woman pays with a Bitcoin wallet on her smartphone, but the transaction is technically unconfirmed until it is mined in a block by a Bitcoin miner. Will the café staff make the woman wait ten minutes until they give her the coffee? What if, because mining is a random process, the next block isn't mined for an hour? The café has two options. It can accept the woman's unconfirmed transaction, but it won't be able to trust the money it received until the next block is mined (Bitcoin's shared ledger hasn't updated yet with the coffee transaction). On the other hand, the café can insist the transaction be added to the Bitcoin blockchain before handing over the cup of coffee. This is a totally unrealistic expectation and has led to a widely used, albeit misinformed, criticism of Bitcoin: the network is too slow to function properly as a medium of commerce. In reality, first-layer Bitcoin transactions are not designed for instant commerce; they are designed to keep an entire global network of peers in perpetual agreement on the status of the Bitcoin ledger. Nevertheless, Bitcoin would eventually shed its moniker as a slow network years later with the advent of the Lightning Network, discussed in the next chapter.

If Bitcoin isn't used for buying coffee, what is it actually used for? Bitcoin is used most crucially by people that prefer a neutral, counterparty-free way to store money. Let's give an example of an individual most empowered by Bitcoin's technology. Imagine a young woman in Nigeria. She lives in a rural village and is a talented graphic designer. If she's able to find freelance work online, she can earn money for her family. But how can she possibly use traditional payment methods to receive money? She doesn't have access to a bank account and wouldn't be able to receive cash in the mail sent via international courier. Bitcoin is actually her best option. Using a smartphone wallet, she can generate a BTC address for herself, send it to a client in Zurich, and receive payment. She doesn't care that the transaction takes ten minutes to confirm; without Bitcoin she wouldn't be able to earn at all. With an example like this, we can see precisely how empowering a technology Bitcoin really is. People in the United States and Europe that have purchased BTC primarily for speculative reasons might be catalyzing worldwide adoption by supporting a growing market value, but people in Latin

America, Africa, and the Middle East with questionable local currencies and unreliable banking industries wholly necessitate a neutral and digital currency such as Bitcoin.

Satoshi's Intent

What exactly was Satoshi Nakamoto trying to accomplish with Bitcoin? For that, we must dive into his writings and correspondences in the early days of the Bitcoin network. He was desperate to provide an alternative not only to financial institutions, but also to currencies prone to devaluation by governments and central banks, an intent that's evident from his early emails and forum posts. On January 3, 2009, the first Bitcoin block ever mined by Satoshi himself included an embedded message instead of transactions (since none existed yet):

> *The Times 03/Jan/2009 Chancellor on brink of second bailout for banks*

Satoshi placed a British newspaper headline about the ongoing financial crisis directly into the ledger's permanent record. By embedding this cryptic message, he speculated that his system for money and transactions offered a necessary evolution and a potential solution to the bailout-prone international banking system.

After Bitcoin had been up and running for a few weeks, Satoshi provided a little more detail on his motivations for the project and demonstrated an acute awareness of the instability of credit-money systems and lower, fractionally reserved layers of the money pyramid:

The root problem with conventional currency is all the trust that's required to make it work. The central bank must be trusted not to debase the currency, but the history of fiat currencies is full of breaches of that trust. Banks must be trusted to hold our money and transfer it electronically, but they lend it out in waves of credit bubbles with barely a fraction in reserve.[23]

Satoshi Nakamoto revealed his ambitions for BTC to exist as a currency denomination, not singularly a payments network. He mentioned *fiat currencies* to refer to currencies issued on the second layer of money by central banks, regardless of what exists on the first; the word *fiat* originally means "by decree" in Latin. Satoshi's criticism of fiat currencies demonstrated a cognizance of the instabilities within our fractionally reserved, layered-money system. In hindsight, the criticism does appear to have motivated him to create Bitcoin. Perhaps the fabricator wanted to provide the world with a new first-layer money that didn't originate from the balance sheet of a central bank.

Visions of Layered Bitcoin

The first vocal advocate for the Bitcoin software after Satoshi Nakamoto was cryptographer Hal Finney. Before Bitcoin's creation and building on the groundwork laid by Adam Back, Finney advanced the application of proof-of-work by designing the *reusable proof-of-work system* used by Satoshi Nakamoto in the design of his software; Finney's contribution to Bitcoin was cemented even before he became a

---

23 *http://p2pfoundation.ning.com/forum/topics/bitcoin-open-source*

Bitcoin user. Finney was Satoshi's earliest and most passionate enthusiast. He was the recipient of the first Bitcoin transaction, when Satoshi sent him 10 BTC on January 12, 2009. Bitcoin was nine days old, and BTC had no price or market value to speak of.

In 2010, Finney provided a particularly fascinating explanation of how Bitcoin layered money might evolve, a prognosis ahead of its time. His quote almost feels like it was custom written for this book:

> *Actually there is a very good reason for Bitcoin-backed banks to exist, issuing their own digital cash currency, redeemable for bitcoins. Bitcoin itself cannot scale to have every single financial transaction in the world be broadcast to everyone and included in the block chain. There needs to be a secondary level of payment systems which is lighter weight and more efficient. Likewise, the time needed for Bitcoin transactions to finalize will be impractical for medium to large value purchases.*
>
> *Bitcoin-backed banks will solve these problems. They can work like banks did before nationalization of currency. Different banks can have different policies, some more aggressive, some more conservative. Some would be fractional reserve while others may be 100% Bitcoin backed. Interest rates may vary. Cash from some banks may trade at a discount to that from others.*
>
> *I believe this will be the ultimate fate of Bitcoin, to be the "high-powered money" that serves as a reserve currency for banks that issue their own digital cash.[24]*

---

24 https://bitcointalk.org/index.php?topic=2500.70;wap2

Let's summarize what Finney is trying to say within the context of layered money. BTC is a slower moving, first-layer money. A few thousand Bitcoin transactions are confirmed in each block, ten minutes apart. For comparison, the major credit card companies process thousands of transactions every second. In order to speed up Bitcoin's velocity, banks will need to own BTC as a first-layer money and issue second-layer deposits that can move more quickly than Bitcoin's chronologically irregular blockchain allows for. A second-layer Bitcoin would allow economic activity without friction. Fractionally reserved, liability-issuing entities will exist, and the market will price each form of second-layer BTC with an according interest rate. Finney was years ahead of Bitcoin's evolution with this prediction, one that time will prove to be the most prescient early words ever written about it. Bitcoin was redefining money and would take its place atop a completely distinct monetary pyramid. Hal Finney passed away in 2014, but his early insight into Bitcoin's potential as world reserve currency echoes in eternity.

CHAPTER 8

LAYERED BITCOIN

It might make sense just to get some in case it catches on. If enough people think the same way, that becomes a self-fulfilling prophecy.
—SATOSHI NAKAMOTO, January 16, 2009

BITCOIN HAS BECOME ITS OWN MONETARY PYRAMID DUE to its properties as a first-layer money. The pyramid is reminiscent of gold-anchored pyramids of the past, but BTC doesn't derive its first-layer status solely from comparisons and metaphors; Satoshi designed a digital asset that specifically mimicked precious metals in order to attract demand. The exponential increase in Bitcoin's market value only reinforces the thesis of its first believers like Hal Finney. Second-layer BTC emerged for the same reasons second-layer gold did. People were willing to hold claims on BTC just as people held claims on gold. The emerging world of digital assets is anchored by BTC in a similar way that the international monetary system was anchored by gold, as described in the first five chapters of this book. BTC is a neutral, counterparty-free money like gold that people trust as a form of final settlement.

This chapter is about the layered BTC-denominated monetary system and how BTC exerts dominance over the entire realm of digital assets.

Owning Physical

Those that strive to own first-layer money often use the phrase "owning physical" to describe the act of owning precious metal in a physical form instead of second-layer gold certificates, shares, or any other promise to pay gold. They are acutely aware of the distinction between first- and second-layer gold and choose to own physical coins and bullion instead of gold substitutes. It comes down to trust: they only trust physical because physical means counterparty-free. Bitcoin has the same international neutrality that gold has; it doesn't depend on any specific people, companies, or countries for it to survive. But Bitcoin has some advantages to gold in the modern age. It exists on computers anywhere and everywhere. It doesn't need to be transported around the world on armored trucks, ships, and airplanes. It also doesn't call for purity testing that enlists expensive equipment, only a Bitcoin node.

Bitcoin's pyramid is anchored by physical ownership of BTC, which begins with the management of Bitcoin private keys. Much like ownership of physical gold relies heavily on vault and security technology, Bitcoin private keys require security precision to avoid loss and theft. The secure and offline storage of BTC is called *cold storage*; implying that private keys are not generated or stored online in *hot wallets*.

Cold storage is a booming business. Fidelity Investments, one of the world's largest financial institutions with over $3 trillion in assets under management, launched its own cold storage subsidiary called Fidelity Digital Assets in 2018 to hold BTC on behalf of large clients. Bitcoin isn't exclusively merging the monetary and cryptography sciences; it's also merging the financial and applied cryptography industries.

We must note that with the introduction of large BTC custodians, their customers will not own first-layer BTC. Customers will own second-layer BTC because they won't be in possession of BTC private keys; the custodian will. As the saying goes among the Bitcoin community, "not your keys, not your coins." And of course, custodians will be subject to government regulation within their jurisdictions. Some governments have proven friendly toward Bitcoin as a new monetary technology, but that stance won't be fully mirrored around the world because of Bitcoin's potential to supplant unstable government currencies.

BTC/USD

There is now a wide array of second-layer BTC money-types. Some instruments mirror the financial arrangements of today's traditional financial system, like deposits. Others are novel and only possible since the inception of Bitcoin. The first examples of second-layer BTC were deposits issued by online BTC/USD exchanges, as shown in Figure 14.

During 2010, the earliest Bitcoin exchanges were formed in order to facilitate trading between BTC and U.S. dollars. They demonstrated something very important about Bitcoin: an active market existed between people that wanted trade between BTC and USD. Bitcoin was designed as a currency

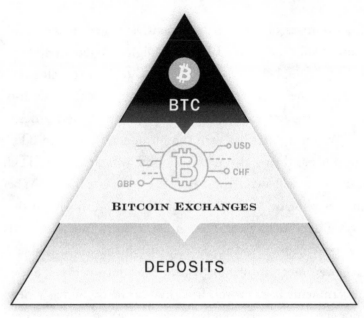

Figure 14

and was being used exactly as intended hardly a year after its genesis. Another common criticism of Bitcoin is that it can't be used to purchase goods or services because most businesses don't accept BTC as a form of payment. This objection misses the point that BTC can be used to purchase the most important commodity of all: money. On exchanges today, BTC buys its owners USD, EUR, and any other major currency they might choose.

An exchange rate between BTC and USD was established in 2010, which bolstered BTC's liquidity and its perception as a new alternative form of money. Customer balances on Bitcoin exchanges were the initial form of second-layer BTC; the balances were claims on BTC but not ownership of private keys themselves. Some exchanges would build stellar reputations by allowing free-flowing BTC withdrawals upon request and having full, not fractional, BTC reserves against all deposits. Others would default on customer balances just like banks had defaulted on deposits over the centuries, whether caused by a cyberattack, theft, or fractional reserves. Despite some early failures, trust in Bitcoin exchanges developed as a cornerstone piece in the Bitcoin monetary puzzle, and almost immediately, the *time value of BTC* presented itself: customers with deposits could lend their collateral to other traders at an interest rate.

Legitimacy

It only took Bitcoin half a decade to achieve legitimacy as a new global currency. Undeniably, it wasn't the darling of governments or the financial industry because of its disruptive and decentralized nature, but it achieved enough market value, venture capital attention, and legal designations to bring it into the mainstream conversation. By 2014, Bitcoin had become a geopolitical force. As the network flourished, it attracted value, study, and investment, which in turn attracted more value. During this period, entrepreneurs started to build an entire infrastructure and industry around Bitcoin because it had become globally accepted as unforgeable digital money. Events in Bitcoin's early history chronicle its quest to become a force of nature and an eradicable fixture in the world of currency.

In its first year, Bitcoin had no value attached to it whatsoever. It didn't have a price, but it did have people that believed in the project and that BTC was worth the electricity, computing power, and effort invested to earn it. This made it money already, as it was a way to store work that had been performed; proof-of-work and Bitcoin mining can be thought of as a form of labor. The highly publicized, earliest Bitcoin transaction occurred when in May 2010, one Bitcoin software developer paid an online acquaintance 10,000 BTC for a $25 Papa John's pizza order, equating to a BTC/USD price of $0.0025. The transaction valued the total market value of BTC at approximately $7,000.[25]

On February 10, 2011, the tech blog *Slashdot* posted an article titled "Online-Only Currency Bitcoin Reaches Dollar Parity." Because of *Slashdot's* popularity among software engineers, many early Bitcoin adopters reference this specific article as the moment they first heard about Bitcoin. After this first slice of internet publicity, barely two years into the project, Bitcoin started to gain serious popularity and attention. A growing community of users all believed in this new monetary form and agreed that the predetermined supply schedule was worth protecting. Soon, enough developers and mind share coalesced around the network, and Satoshi bid adieu. As of this writing, the estimated one million BTC that he mined during the first year of Bitcoin's existence has never been transacted.

The total market value of BTC passed $100 million in June 2011 around the same time as the website *Gawker* published an article titled "The Underground Website Where You Can Buy Any Drug Imaginable." The Silk Road was an online black market, most widely used for the buying and

---

25 *Total market value of BTC = BTC/USD price × current BTC supply*

selling of illegal drugs on the Internet. As a new, online, decentralized digital currency not yet on the radar of law enforcement, BTC was the perfect currency for Silk Road users. In Bitcoin, there was no bank that could flag suspicious transactions, no cash that had to be sent through the mail or exchanged in person, and conveniently no law enforcement to monitor the Bitcoin ledger for transactions. Without anybody looking, Bitcoin transactions might as well have been anonymous. The *Gawker* article explained that one must first go to a Bitcoin exchange to purchase BTC in order to participate in this online marketplace:

> *As for transactions, Silk Road doesn't accept credit cards, PayPal, or any other form of payment that can be traced or blocked. The only money good here is Bitcoins.*

The Federal Bureau of Investigations eventually opened an inquiry and shut down the Silk Road. The FBI seized BTC during its operation and faced new truths about money in the digital era. From that point on, law enforcement from around the world began to monitor Bitcoin's ledger for suspicious activity in order to hunt down criminals. Law enforcement developed ways to associate Bitcoin transactions with internet location data in order to do this. After law enforcement agencies started monitoring the Bitcoin ledger, Bitcoin was no longer the ideal currency for criminal activity, rather far from it. This disassociation boosted the legitimacy of Bitcoin in a pivotal way.

On November 28, 2012, Bitcoin's first *halving* event took place after its 210,000th block was mined and the mining reward for each block "halved" from 50 BTC to 25 BTC. While the moment passed without any flare or drama from a blockchain perspective, it was paramount from a monetary one. When Satoshi designed the first working version of the Bitcoin software code, he outlined a monetary policy that stretched out over a century into the future. Then after four years in existence, Bitcoin's network experienced its first supply adjustment without drama, greed, or objection from any of its participants. The predetermined supply schedule, a supply halving after each epoch, and a maximum total supply of 21 million BTC were all stipulations of the network that were observed, not questioned. Satoshi had invented non-discretionary monetary policy wherein human discretion could never alter the supply algorithm of Bitcoin. The awareness of this awe-inspiring invention and strength of consensus drove an investment thesis for Bitcoin; it was a currency that couldn't be expanded in supply or devalued. Bitcoin had arrived as digital gold.

In 2013, the price of BTC/USD exploded, rising above $1,000 and giving the network a total market value of $10 billion. The *Financial Times*, *Wall Street Journal*, and *Bloomberg* started publishing articles about Bitcoin and the growing cryptocurrency industry with regularity, and Bitcoin's brand started to gain recognition. Government officials likely belittled the idea of decentralized cryptocurrency because Bitcoin's lack of a central issuer had stoked a discussion about the separation between money and governments.

Bitcoin officially gained recognition in the eyes of the United States government in 2014, progressing toward legitimacy and past the ugly brushstrokes left by the Silk Road era. The IRS determined that ownership of BTC was to be treated as property and that gains realized in USD terms were subject to capital gain taxes. This was an admission by the U.S. government that owning BTC was an unmistakable form of property like real estate or physical gold and should be taxed as such.

Additionally, the U.S. commodity futures regulator ruled that Bitcoin was indeed a commodity and not a currency. It compared Bitcoin to gold in its own research process and concluded that ownership of BTC is possession of a numerical commodity due to the software's reliance on private keys. Bitcoin was starting to morph into its own asset class, despite being difficult to define in the traditional context because of its novel characteristics.

By 2014, even the U.S. government was fully aware of the monetary evolution taking place. Bitcoin attracted savers in countries with poor governing stability and property rights who desired a borderless, seizure-resistant money. It attracted savers within a dollar denomination that had lost faith in the Federal Reserve as a source of monetary discipline. Bona fide demand for Bitcoin existed throughout every corner of the planet. In 2017, Bitcoin's total market value exploded past $100 billion in its most dramatic price surge yet. The exponential growth of Bitcoin had become undeniable.

Tulips

During the seventeenth century and a few decades after the founding of the Bank of Amsterdam, a speculative price bubble occurred in Dutch tulip bulbs. As a beautiful luxury item, tulips became all the rage in the Netherlands as everybody wanted a piece of the highly coveted commodity. Prices of bulbs exploded and then collapsed shortly thereafter, as all speculative bubbles do. The word *bubble* would be used throughout history to describe increases in the price of an asset that seemed unfathomable to many, increases that would unquestionably and consistently end in ruinous decline. Of course, many have fruitlessly tried to associate the word *bubble* with Bitcoin.

Bitcoin's exponential price rise since its birth continues to bring about cries of a bubble and comparisons to Dutch tulips despite having fully recovered from intimidating 80% price declines now on *three* separate occasions. The BTC/USD price is breathtakingly volatile, far outstretching price fluctuations we typically see across other asset classes. Its volatility, however, is not a reflection of asset quality or even excellence. If Bitcoin truly is to grow from an adolescent monetary network to the basis of an international monetary system, surely the ups and downs on its way will mimic a formidable rollercoaster. If the market value of BTC were to equal the market value of all the world's gold, the BTC/USD price would reach approximately $500,000.[26] It is safe to assume that the journey from less than $1 to $500,000

---

26 *Assuming a $10 trillion total market value for gold and approximately 20 million BTC (estimated supply in 2025)*

would come with its fair share of frenetic price swings, both up and down. These vacillations are ingrained into Bitcoin's maturation and will separate early adopters from those who will wait for the price to stabilize in USD terms. None of this volatility, however, precludes BTC from being a store of value and an alternative to currencies based on aging archetypes.

In reality, Bitcoin is nothing like the Dutch tulip mania. Bubbles don't burst three times in a decade and come back stronger each resurgence, and the investing public is finally waking up to this fact. In 2020, some of the most legendary hedge fund investors of this generation, Paul Tudor Jones and Stanley Druckenmiller, acknowledged ownership of BTC. Investment management powerhouses such as AllianceBernstein, Blackrock, and Fidelity Investments made public recommendations for clients to have BTC in their portfolios as a hedge against the devaluation or demise of government currencies. PayPal, the world's largest online payment processor, gave its 300 million global customers the ability to purchase BTC on its platform. It began to become clear to the investing community that denying Bitcoin's place in the future of money was like denying the Internet's place in the future of commerce in 1999. Internet stocks might have experienced a speculative price bubble at the turn of the twenty-first century, but the world's biggest publicly traded corporations today are Microsoft, Apple, Amazon, Alphabet (Google), and Facebook, which have generated trillions of dollars in market value thanks to the Internet.

The flurry of endorsements preceded the BTC/USD price reaching a new all-time high at the beginning of 2021 as the total market value eclipsed $600 billion. What was once a digital token attached to a hobbyist software worth less than a penny in 2010 had become a $34,000 commodity only a decade later. The famous $25 Papa John's pizza trade would be worth $340 million on Bitcoin's twelfth birthday, January 3, 2021. Figure 15 shows the meteoric rise in BTC's total market value since 2010.

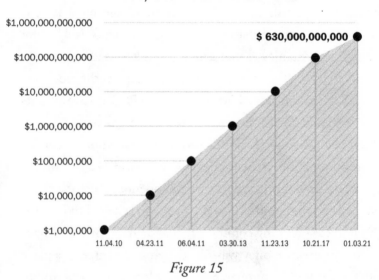

BTC/USD Total Market Value

Figure 15

Lightning Network

Lightning Network is a technological enhancement to Bitcoin that positively transforms it from a slower-moving commodity like physical gold to a currency moving at lightspeed. And the key ingredient to the Lightning Network is the smart contract. Generally, *smart contracts* are programmable agreements capable of anything that can be coded into software. For the objective of Bitcoin, smart contracts are most importantly capable of escrow and multiple-party coordination. The smart contracts in Lightning Network, Hashed TimeLock Contracts (HTLCs), have scaled Bitcoin into a monetary network capable of processing millions of transactions per second. Let's take a closer look at how Lightning Network evolved.

In the first couple years of the Bitcoin network, a small contingent of Bitcoin enthusiasts contributed their own ideas and improvements to the project. They fixed some critical vulnerabilities that could have abruptly ended the network before it caught momentum. These software engineers and cryptographers worked on Bitcoin because they had conviction in the technology, owned BTC, and wanted the network to succeed. They weren't receiving an income from any employer; they were working out of belief in a new denomination. Over the years, they graduated Bitcoin from a project to a legitimate global monetary network.

The most crucial updates that transitioned Bitcoin to a smart contract platform occurred from 2015 to 2017. These Bitcoin Improvement Proposals (BIPs) turned one-dimensional Bitcoin transactions into wildly customizable financial contracts, without changing any of Bitcoin's fundamental rules.[27]

In 2016, a paper from software engineers Joseph Poon and Thaddeus Dryja called "The Bitcoin Lightning Network:

---

27 *Check Lock Time Verify (BIP 65), CheckSequenceVerify (BIP 68, 112, 113), and Segregated Witness (BIP 141, 143, 147)*

Scalable Off-Chain Instant Payments" built upon all the smart contract innovation happening on the Bitcoin software. The paper was a proposal for a new type of Bitcoin smart contract (HTLCs) that enabled instantly settling payments *without having to wait for the next block to be mined.* Lightning Network not only infinitely increases Bitcoin's capability as a medium of exchange but also allows for innovations such as paying for online streaming by the millisecond. And in the digital age of streaming everything, why shouldn't money stream as well?

Lightning Network also brings a new dimension to the time value of BTC. Users that provide BTC as collateral to Lightning Network in order to facilitate transactions can potentially earn income from providing this liquidity. This is a historically unprecedented way to earn a return on capital without ever relinquishing custody of it because collateral providers don't actually part ways with their BTC when dedicating it to Lightning Network. Interest rates derived from this type of activity could function as a reference rate in the Bitcoin world because of Lightning Network's uniquely counterparty-free nature. The very concept of the *time value of money* is changing as these new technologies permeate the monetary landscape.

Alternative Cryptocurrencies

Bitcoin copycats were inevitable. Bitcoin is a free and open-source software, which means that the software is free to download and open to view by anybody. On multiple occasions, Bitcoin has resisted fundamental changes to its rulebook from developers that were out of consensus with the majority of Bitcoin users. Alternative versions of cryptocurrency to Bitcoin emerged, whether copied directly, tweaked, or reimagined. If ideas better than Bitcoin existed, capital would gravitate toward these alternatives and away from Bitcoin. So far, however, no cryptocurrency has challenged BTC over any sustained duration, measured in both market value and hashpower. Alternative cryptocurrencies exist on a lower layer within the BTC money pyramid due to a price relationship, much like national currencies existed on a layer below the dollar after the Bretton Woods agreement of 1944. Like the USD acts as the base price for currencies from around the world, BTC acts as a base price for all digital currencies.

BTC also acts as a monetary constraint on lower layers of its own pyramid because it's unforgeable, but this doesn't prevent the issuance of second-layer BTC or any other digital asset. Whether classified as copycats or money-grabs, a volcano of cryptocurrencies erupted after the early success of Bitcoin. Exchanges added cryptocurrencies to their platforms which notably traded against BTC, not USD, as their base currency. A new asset class of digital token-based currencies is here, and BTC functions as the final form of settlement within that digital realm.

BTC will never be alone as a digital asset; it will always have both ancillary and auxiliary assets. But it is the one unit of account on which others in the digital universe can rely on for incorruptibility. The Bitcoin protocol's dominance as the primary value-transfer protocol of the Internet will likely endure for decades to come, much like how the Transmission

Control Protocol, Internet Protocol, and Hypertext Transfer Protocol (TCP/IP/HTTP) dominate our digital interactions every day when we connect to the Internet or browse the web.

Stablecoins

A rapidly growing second layer within Bitcoin's monetary pyramid is a new type of digital asset called stablecoins. *Stablecoins* are liabilities issued in the form of digital tokens by private sector companies. These stablecoins are supposed to trade at a "stable" value relative to dollars, for example. The moniker of "stable" is a bit of an oxymoron in this case because as we've learned, monetary instruments on lower layers of money rarely possess enduring stability. Stablecoins: digital coins that are stable until they aren't.

Stablecoins were invented because exchanges needed an easier and quicker way for customers to convert between BTC and USD. In essence, exchanges create their own cryptocurrencies that represent USD in a bank account but are transacted with private keys and addresses just like Bitcoin.

The most famous stablecoin is one that has yet to launch: Facebook's Diem (originally called Libra). Its intent is to be backed by U.S. Treasury Bills and other dollar-denominated monetary instruments. Whether or not Diem launches, Facebook's announcement of a stablecoin in 2019 was a major landmark for digital money. The moment Facebook attempted to encroach upon the world of money was the moment central banks knew they needed a formal response to the merger of money and cryptography. Private sector banks are also looking to capitalize on the demand for dollar-pegged, ledger-based digital tokens: J.P. Morgan launched its own stablecoin, called JPM Coin, in 2020.

In January 2021, the U.S. Treasury issued a definitive guidance on the legality of cryptocurrencies and stablecoins in a report from the Office of the Comptroller of the Currency (OCC).[28] The guidance names both cryptocurrencies and distributed ledgers *independent node verification networks* (*INVNs*), formally defines the word "stablecoin" exactly as we have in this section, and approves both of them for use by banks to digitally transact value as long as banking laws are followed. The ruling was proof that the future monetary rails would be built with the backbone of cryptography:

> *We therefore conclude that a bank may validate, store, and record payments transactions by serving as a node on an INVN. Likewise, a bank may use INVNs and related stablecoins to carry out other permissible payment activities. A bank must conduct these activities consistent with applicable law and safe and sound banking practices.*

Commodity Futures

Though New York is the banking capital of the United States, Chicago has always been its commodity hedging capital. During the nineteenth century, Chicago standardized the world of forward and futures contracts, allowing farmers to contractually sell their crop before it harvested. In 1898, standardization of butter and egg futures contracts led to the formation of the Chicago Butter and Egg Board, the predecessor

---

28 OCC, *Interpretive Letter 1174.*

to the Chicago Mercantile Exchange (CME), which today is the world's largest derivatives exchange. The CME would add practically every commodity imaginable to its range of futures products over the years, from live cattle futures in 1964, to silver futures in 1969, to Bitcoin futures in 2017.

In 2016, when the CME announced plans to publish Bitcoin price data in preparation for a launch of Bitcoin futures the following year, the weight of Chicago as the worldwide authority on commodities was thrown behind Bitcoin and significantly added to its legitimacy. CME Bitcoin futures help financial market participants translate between BTC and USD, which will directly contribute to Bitcoin's adoption. Businesses can engage in BTC-denominated activity knowing that they can actively manage away unwanted exchange rate risk. Additionally, Bitcoin futures offer a second-layer BTC to participants that operate only within the dollar pyramid and simply want exposure to changes in the price of BTC, not possession of Bitcoin private keys. CME's product brought Bitcoin forward on its path to full integration with the traditional financial system.

Layered Bitcoin

As worldwide adoption of Bitcoin as a currency and as a monetary mindset continue, Bitcoin's second layer is blossoming with a variety of BTC-based promises, alternative cryptocurrencies, and stablecoins. Figure 16 shows that Bitcoin is at the top of its own novel monetary pyramid, with some second-layer monies stemming from balance sheets and others from price relationships.

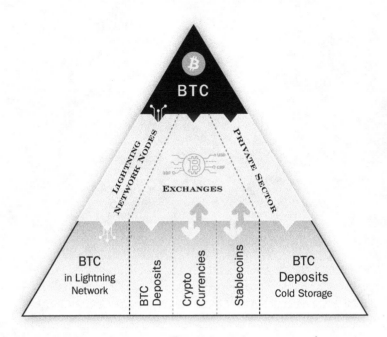

Figure 16

CHAPTER 9

CENTRAL BANK DIGITAL CURRENCIES

T HE INVENTION OF BITCOIN HAS CHANGED MONEY FOR-
ever and forced central banks to respond with their own
iteration of cryptocurrency. Worldwide, central banks are preparing to launch *central bank digital currencies* (*CBDCs*) as
another second-layer monetary instrument originating from
their balance sheets on par with reserves and paper currency.
But nobody quite knows how CBDCs will be constructed,
how similar or different their technology will be to Bitcoin's,
or the impact they'll have. This chapter will look at where central banks are in the process of launching their crypto-com-
petitors, and speculate on the interaction between CBDCs,
stablecoins, and Bitcoin in the future.

Change the Game

Central bankers of the Federal Reserve and an economic
brain trust from around the world have gathered in Jackson
Hole, Wyoming since 1982 to evolve the science and practice

of central banking. At the 2019 symposium, then Governor of the Bank of England Mark Carney made a speech that delivered a dire message about the international monetary and financial system: "In the longer-term, we need to change the game." He bemoaned a unipolar currency regime in which the dollar is the sole reserve currency as unsustainable and gave life to the exploration of a post-dollar metamorphosis of money. The problem is that with long-term changes potentially decades away, planning for them becomes an overwhelming task. Laying new tracks for money's future is easier said than done.

Helicopter Money

In 2016, Ben Broadbent, a senior Bank of England official, delivered a speech titled "Central Banks and Digital Currencies" at the London School of Economics that must also be catalogued into monetary history. The speech sought to touch on the following questions:

> *What is the key innovation in private-sector digital currencies such as bitcoin? What is a 'central bank digital currency'? And what might be the economic implications of introducing one?*

The speech tried to grapple with the magnitude of Bitcoin's innovation and its implications for how we think of currency, and it also took the conversation forward by admitting that central banks could use the idea of a token-based digital cash like Bitcoin to their own benefit by widening access to who all could hold central bank liabilities, or second-layer money.

What is the attraction of central bankers to issuing their own digital currencies? The answer lies in wider access to second-layer money. Recall that the Federal Reserve issues two types of money, wholesale reserves for private sector banks and retail cash for people. In order to provide monetary stimulus, the Fed issues reserves and hopes that private sector banks will use those reserves to circulate third-layer deposits into the economy by lending money. With a CBDC, the Fed could issue second-layer money directly to people in the form of digital helicopter money; the phrase "helicopter money" comes from Milton Friedman, who in 1969 provided the imagery of dropping cash out of a helicopter in order to stimulate economic demand.

The Fed wouldn't necessarily be able to provide this type of economic stimulus without a larger political debate; a CBDC blurs the line between the central bank's independent monetary policy and government-controlled fiscal policy. Helicopter money has been explored as a monetary policy tool for decades, and with the popularity of political ideas such as Universal Basic Income, CBDCs are the ideal vehicle to transmit direct payments to citizens in the future.

Broadbent formally introduced the CBDC acronym that is sure to dominate the monetary conversation for many years to come. Since his speech, the central banks of China, Sweden, and Australia have started testing CBDCs. The European Central Bank, Bank of England, and Federal Reserve are all several years into their research efforts and have all indicated that a form of central bank digital currency is likely to arrive in the coming years. The question of whether or not CBDCs are coming is moot.

The current reality is that there are more questions than answers surrounding central bank digital currencies and the path they will follow. Will they be retail second-layer money to which the entire public has access? If that is the case, what happens to banks and their issuance of third-layer money to the public? After all, the public uses third-layer bank deposits as its primary form of money, and a retail CBDC has the potential to supplant third-layer deposits as the preferred money-type for citizens. And from a societal standpoint, how will central banks use the new powers of surveillance and monetary policy that would emanate from the issuance of publicly accessible digital currencies? Central banks around the world are consulting industry and society on how to answer these questions about the world of digital money.

CBDC Design

Without any official characteristics yet, CBDCs are unchartered monetary territory. From a layered-money perspective however, CBDCs are more defined. When issued by a central bank, digital currency will be a second-layer money, a liability on the central bank's balance sheet alongside cash notes and reserves. The world is looking for a new multipolar game to play as Mark Carney said, and nations that want to participate in the overhaul must build their digital currencies with specific characteristics.

Central banks first have to decide which liability they want their digital currencies to emulate more: wholesale reserves or retail cash. The conversation demands a layered-money context in order to achieve clarity around this important and foundational decision for digital currency issuance.

When people use cash, they are using second-layer money and avoiding the banking layer altogether. But most people don't use cash anymore. They use bank deposits and payment platforms linked to bank accounts for their daily interaction with money, which occurs on the third and lower layers. Central banks are wary of the effects on the banking industry of launching digital currencies. With this new technology, they have the opportunity to actively reduce the role of banks in the issuance of money; if CBDCs are accessible to the entire populace, people might reduce their reliance on bank accounts to receive direct deposits and pay bills.

Alternatively, central banks could issue a digital currency in the form of wholesale reserves, which would only be accessible to banks. The digital reserves option has the potential to modernize financial infrastructure for the banking system, but it won't impact how society interacts with money.

Will central banks issue a retail CBDC or a wholesale CBDC? We'll see some attempt one or the other, and some attempt both. A wholesale CBDC doesn't bring into question the displacement of banks. It's also probably the best way for central banks to test new technology in a live environment with select banks as users instead of with millions of people. A retail CBDC has the potential to change the concept of monetary policy itself by giving central banks the ability to interact with people directly instead of only with other banks. Different central banks will choose different paths.

China

Geopolitical tensions between China and the United States have risen over the past several years and will continue to do so as China fosters its desire to be the world's superpower. Through its Belt and Road initiative, a worldwide trade infrastructure network with over one hundred nations participating, China is spreading its influence and its currency denomination across the globe.

But China's rise is unquestionably missing a corresponding deep and liquid capital market for its currency denomination, especially when it comes to a risk-free asset. China's government bond market is but a blip on the international radar of liquid and safe securities, but more importantly, China's currency denomination renminbi (RMB, "people's currency") which began with the founding of the People's Bank of China in 1948, is not a freely traded currency. Trade between RMB and other currencies is largely restricted by the Chinese government, exchange rates are managed instead of market-driven, and convertibility between RMB and the world's reserve currency, USD, is far from seamless. The renminbi, despite all recent attempts by China at internationalizing the currency, remains a closed capital account. This means that companies and banks can't freely move renminbi in and out of the country, negating any demand for RMB as a world reserve currency. Nevertheless, China is preparing for a post-dollar world. During the few years after the 2008 financial crisis, China instituted direct cross-currency relationships with some of its allies in order to reduce its dependence on using the USD as a clearing mechanism for international trade. This started with China's 2011 agreement with Russia and continued as it looked for alternatives to the global dollar standard.

The People's Bank of China is already live-testing a digital renminbi system called Digital Currency Electronic Payment (DCEP) in select cities with a limited number of citizens and businesses participating in the first stage of the rollout. China is moving forward with an entire legal framework for DCEP as it looks to jump out ahead in the global CBDC race that is only just beginning. China will likely use its digital RMB as a tool to grow its global influence and spread the adoption of its denomination. When fully implemented, DCEP carries the potential to be the largest financial surveillance operation in the world, especially if it forces its major trading partners into using DCEP to transact with Chinese entities. One of the most important details of China's legal framework interestingly forbids the issuance of RMB-backed digital tokens by private sector banks, or RMB stablecoins. This will be a distinguishing trait of China's CBDC, as China might be transitioning to a financial system without third-layer bank deposits and drive all of its citizens into its second-layer retail CBDC instead.

Digital Euro

The European Central Bank published a "Report on a Digital Euro" in October 2020 and demonstrated full intent to take its currency denomination digital. The report concluded that a "digital euro may even become essential in a number of possible scenarios," an admission that the merger of the monetary and cryptography sciences is official and fundamentally changing the world's monetary order. The report is filled with more questions than answers about the digital euro, like how a CBDC would impact the second- and third-layer relationship between the ECB and European private sector banks, whether it would coexist with paper currency or replace it altogether, and what it would mean for monetary policy itself. Private sector banks are threatened by CBDCs because of their potential to displace the demand for bank deposits, and the ECB appears eager to strike the right balance. According to the report, the ECB seems ready to launch a digital euro project and full technical exploration phase in 2021.

Fedcoin

Current Federal Reserve chair Jerome Powell addressed a possible Fedcoin, a nickname given to the Federal Reserve's prospective digital currency, during an International Monetary Fund conference in 2020:

> It's more important for the United States to get it right than to be first. We are committed to carefully and thoughtfully evaluating the potential costs and benefits of a central bank digital currency for the U.S. economy and payments system. We have not made a decision to issue a CBDC.

Although no concrete plans exist for Fedcoin, the Federal Reserve is clearly on track to create one in due course, if not because of the continued success of Bitcoin, then due to the sudden realization that it might be the last major central

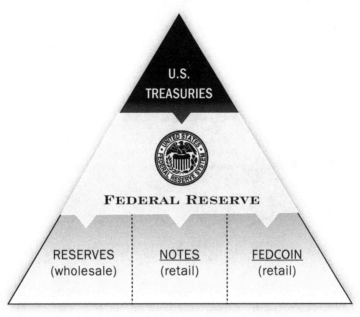

Figure 17

bank in the world to release one. The Fed, based on indications from China and Europe, is already going to be late to the CBDC party. It is unlikely to issue a retail CBDC that could be used by the public as a form of digital notes right away; instead, it will conceivably create a form of digital bank reserves in order to test the technology before eventually launching a publicly available, retail-facing Fedcoin. Figure 17 shows how a Fedcoin would be a second-layer money alongside reserves and cash.

BTC and CBDC Price Relationship

The underlying thesis of this book is that BTC will stand alone on the first-layer of money in the future. If only one word about Bitcoin could be used to describe why, we'd have

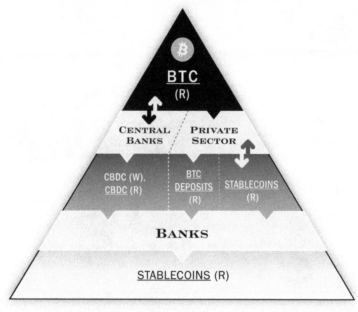

Figure 18

to choose one coined only a few years ago in 2014 by author and seminal economic thinker Nassim Nicholas Taleb: *antifragile*. Here is how Taleb defined it:

> *Some things benefit from shocks; they thrive and grow when exposed to volatility, randomness, disorder, and stressors and love adventure, risk, and uncertainty. Yet, in spite of the ubiquity of the phenomenon, there is no word for the exact opposite of fragile. Let us call it antifragile. Antifragility is beyond resilience or robustness. The resilient resists shocks and stays the same; the antifragile gets better.*

Bitcoin is antifragile because it thrives off global monetary disorder within the dollar pyramid and is resilient to the threats, slander, and legislation from dismissive bureaucratic entities. The plain truth about Bitcoin is that nobody controls it. It has become the first-ever government-free, universally accessible digital currency. And for these reasons, all currencies in the purely digital realm will face price discovery in BTC terms. This means that all digital currencies, from cryptocurrencies to CBDCs, will be measured in BTC, just like the Bretton Woods agreement in 1944 mandated all currencies be measured in USD. Figure 18 elucidates a future in which BTC is the world reserve currency and *only* first-layer money.

In order for this type of BTC-denominated layered money system to evolve, a few technological details need to fall into place that might sound far-fetched but are already in development within central banks today. The last piece of the puzzle on the path to BTC becoming world reserve currency will be the atomic swap.

Atomic Swaps

Understanding the atomic swap and its role in the future of money requires the amalgamation of three elements discussed in this book: Lightning Network, Hashed TimeLock Contracts (HTLCs), and Distributed Ledger Technology (DLT). We'll quickly review the key aspects of each, and then show how they all fit together. Lightning Network is a network of BTC users that can transact instantly with each other instead of having to wait ten minutes for the next block to be mined. This is possible thanks to smart contracts called HTLCs. Separately, Distributed Ledger Technology (DLT) is a term that mainstream academia and central bank research departments use to describe Bitcoin-inspired software.

Now here's how all the terms are bound together. DLT software equipped with HTLCs that are compatible with Bitcoin's Lightning Network will be used by central banks to launch their CBDCs. If the smart contracts are compatible across digital assets, it would enable a world of atomic swaps.

An *atomic swap* is, at its core, a trade. It's a smart contract that allows for the trade between digital currencies without using a third-party exchange. This is absolutely revolutionary in the world of finance and trading, and let's use an example of buying shares of Apple to illustrate why. Say you want to purchase 100 shares of Apple at $100 each. You deposit $10,000 into a stock exchange. Those wanting to sell their shares will deposit them as well. The exchange is required in this situation to ensure that both the buyer and the seller have the money and assets necessary to complete the trade. Without a third party, traders would have to trust each other every time they traded. But with an exchange, that is not the case.

Atomic swaps fundamentally change these basic ideas of trading. They are programmed to execute the trade for both parties or for neither, eliminating counterparty risk, exchange risk, and default risk altogether. It's important to understand that atomic swaps will only work on central bank digital currencies that are built using DLT software outfitted with the same type of smart contracts present in Bitcoin's Lightning Network. However, this doesn't necessarily mean that a central bank issuing a CBDC on a distributed ledger would cede any control over the underlying currency.

Several implementations of DLT already allow for atomic swaps. Here is a real-life example of the work being done on atomically swappable central bank digital currencies. In 2019, the Monetary Authority of Singapore, the Bank of Canada, JP Morgan, and Accenture announced a successful atomic swap between Canadian dollars (CAD) and Singapore dollars (SGD) across two separate DLT platforms using HTLCs "without the need for a third party that is trusted by both jurisdictions." The transaction's setup was incredibly complicated from a software programming and computer science standpoint and took much time and care to execute, but this is the type of research monetary authorities around the world are conducting right now to explore the future of money. The Canadian central bank used a DLT called Corda, and Singapore's central bank used a DLT called Quorum, both solutions offered as products by private enterprises. The two DLTs have several fundamental differences but are compatible where it counts: they allow for HTLCs with each other. Central banks will need an increasingly large applied-cryptography contingent amongst their senior ranks in order to iron out all the technical details to CBDC implementation. Whether they decide to use a banking software solution, an alternative cryptocurrency, or Bitcoin itself, central banks have an array of options when it comes to their ultimate launch of digital currencies. If central banks want their digital currencies to thrive in the Bitcoin era, they will issue CBDCs that use DLT software with HTLC capabilities in order to join the atomic swap club. With BTC as the only first-layer digital currency, every other digital currency, no matter how powerful the issuer, will ultimately be measured against BTC.

CHAPTER 10

FREEDOM OF CURRENCY DENOMINATION

S INCE THE CREATION OF THE BANK OF AMSTERDAM IN the seventeenth century, monetary instruments and governments have been linked to each other. But in the digital age, money and state don't necessarily mix anymore. To many, the entire concept of government money is becoming obsolete as the rise of Bitcoin bellows in antithesis. Because Bitcoin is software, mathematics, and speech, it should be considered a human right. Bitcoin embodies freedom of currency denomination because it gives people the ability to denominate their earnings and savings away from government association. Whether people have changed their unit of account to BTC from their local currencies because of political ideals, nonviolent protest, or a belief that technology enables a novel form of money, they are naturally endowed with the freedom to choose how the fruits of their labor are measured. Bitcoin gives people around the world the first genuine alternative to their national currencies, a trend which is impossible to reverse now that over 100 million people own it globally.

A Vision of the Future

Here's an outline of how our monetary future might play out in the context of layered money. Today, central banks employ trading desks in order to buy and sell their currency in the foreign exchange market in hopes to maintain exchange rate stability. In the near future, they'll add BTC trading capabilities to their open market operations in hopes to guide their digital currency's exchange rate in BTC terms.

Bitcoin has caused a seismic shift in the monetary balance of power away from governments, even as central bank digital currencies wait in the wings. China will launch its CBDC in preparation for the 2022 Winter Olympics. The European Central Bank, Federal Reserve, and other major central banks will be testing CBDCs by then and will follow with launches of their own.

Banks will issue stablecoins that offer advantages to holding CBDCs, such as higher interest rates or cash-back membership benefits. If friction is minimal when trading between one digital currency and another thanks to atomic swaps, the stablecoin universe will thrive as the source of credit elasticity, or lending. Banks will issue loans, record them as assets on their balance sheet, and issue stablecoins instead of deposits as liabilities. Banks can dramatically increase transparency and rejuvenate trustworthiness by using DLT, and transition to a dynamic balance sheet that allows the investing public to see live capital ratios instead of heavily window-dressed static quarterly reporting. In order to join the monetary order of the future, banks must issue stablecoins that are atomically swappable with other stablecoins, CBDCs, and BTC.

Banks will become masters of the atomic swap, making markets between digital currencies in order to pursue arbitrage and generate profit. With atomic swaps and instant settlement between digital currencies, a path forward exists for the transition to a Bitcoin-anchored monetary system.

Governments and corporations around the world will purchase BTC and hold it as a cash reserve because it reduces reliance on the current dollar system, indicating that the era of global dollar denomination is eroding in the direction of cryptocurrency, instead of any other government currency like the renminbi or euro. Gold will continue to serve as a trusted neutral money, but it has no realistic capability to serve as the rails for a digital financial system. This is not to dismiss gold as the best form of counterparty-free money the world has ever known: Bitcoin has *only* captured 6% of gold's total worldwide market value. Furthermore, gold's international monetary role has returned with a vengeance since 2007; central banks around the world have increased gold asset holdings dramatically as a hedge to the dollar system's instability and fragility. Gold is considered an insurance on monetary disorder and disarray, one that tends to work best during earthquakes in the dollar pyramid. But gold's physicality falls short in a digital world where Bitcoin thrives. Eventually, Bitcoin will likely replace gold as the most desired neutral money and exceed it in total market value.

For the public, all money will be digital tokens that will be held in digital wallets. People will simultaneously hold an assortment of currencies: BTC for a neutrality, CBDCs for paying taxes and collecting benefits, and stablecoins for earning interest. Many will rely on second-layer CBDCs and do away with third-layer bank deposits altogether. A growing number of people will survive exclusively on non-government cryptocurrencies like BTC and never subject themselves to counterparty risk.

Money of Choice

Our multipolar world is looking for a monetary rebirth, and Bitcoin offers exactly that. Countries will resist, and some central bankers and politicians will succeed at keeping Bitcoin out of their countries because it threatens their power. But freedom of currency denomination will eventually emerge, whether it comes from banking havens in Europe, offshore money centers in the Caribbean, or the United States of America itself. Gone will be the days when an individual only uses the currency of the country where he or she resides. No currency in the digital realm will ever be able to prove itself as resistant to corruption as BTC, wherein transactions once confirmed are impossible to override, making Bitcoin the ultimate tool of financial freedom anywhere in the world. Bitcoin is where the Internet collides with money to bring about change in the same transformative way it did with communication and commerce.

Looking back at Bitcoin's origin through a layered lens, we can see that a new first-layer money had been invented. It was something the world desperately needed, and we are only beginning to understand its impact. In the future, the currency you use will not merely reflect your birthplace or country of residence, but your preferences. Use this map of layered money to emancipate yourself from the boundaries of traditional finance and explore a world of currencies without geographical confinements. Reference the layered money design to see exactly where your money exists in the monetary landscape and empower yourself to achieve freedom of currency denomination by navigating toward your money of choice.

ACKNOWLEDGEMENTS

Thank you to my wife Chandni for joining me in this journey. Thank you to my parents for always encouraging me to follow my dreams, and to Jay and Kashvi for their unwavering support. Thank you to my trusted team of editors/contributors for helping me make this book become a reality: my wife, my dad, "360", Vikram Amritraj, Sarah Tsai, Stephen Cole, Jason Don, Nic Carter, Jeremy and Nikita McWells, and Prakash Amritraj. Thank you to my copyeditor and publishing consultant Cathy Suter for her invaluable contributions. Thank you to the talented Anton Khodakovsky for the book's cover and graphics. Thank you to those who trusted me as a fiduciary and gave me the opportunity to trade the U.S. Treasury market at the highest level. Thank you to Professor Perry Mehrling for his paper *The Inherent Hierarchy of Money* upon which the Layered Money framework was built. Thank you to Zoltan Pozsar for his research on the "Money Matrix." Thank you to Jeff Snider for his eye-opening research on Eurodollars. Thank you to Nas for inspiring me as a writer. And finally, thank you to everybody who read *The Time Value of Bitcoin*.

REFERENCES

Agueci, Paul, Leyla Alkan, Adam Copeland, Isaac Davis, Antoine Martin, Kate Pingitore, Caroline Prugar, Tyisha Rivas. "A Primer on the GCF Repo® Service," *Federal Reserve Bank of New York Staff Reports*, no. 671, April 2014, revised May 2014. https://www.newyorkfed.org/medialibrary/media/research/staff_reports/sr671.pdf

Bagehot, Walter. *Lombard Street: A Description of the Money Market*. New York: Scribner, Armstrong & Co, 1873.

Bank of Canada and Monetary Authority of Singapore. Jasper–Ubin Design Paper, "Enabling Cross-Border High Value Transfer Using Distributed Ledger Technologies," 2019. https://www.accenture.com/_acnmedia/PDF-99/Accenture-Cross-Border-Distributed-Ledger-Technologies.pdf

Bank of International Settlements. "Central bank digital currencies: foundational principles and core features, Bank of Canada, European Central Bank, Bank of Japan, Sveriges Riksbank, Swiss National Bank, Bank of England." Board of Governors Federal Reserve System, Bank for International Settlements. Report no. 1, 2020. https://www.bis.org/publ/othp33.pdf

Bao, Cecilia and Emma Paine. "Insights from the Federal Reserve's Weekly Balance Sheet, 1942–1975," *Studies in Applied Economics*, no.104, 2018. Johns Hopkins Institute for Applied Economics, Global Health, and the Study of Business Enterprise.

Bao, Cecilia, Justin Chen, Nicholas Fries, Andrew Gibson, Emma Paine and Kurt Schuler. "The Federal Reserve's Weekly Balance Sheet since 1914," *Studies in Applied Economics*, no.115, 2018. John's Hopkins Institute for Applied Economics, Global Health, and the Study of Business Enterprise.

Blandin, Apolline, Dr. Gina Pieters, Yue Wu, Thomas Eisermann, Anton Dek, Sean Taylor, Damaris Njoki. "3rd Global Cryptoasset Benchmarking Study," Cambridge Centre for Alternative Finance (CCAF) at the University of Cambridge Judge Business School, September 2020. https://www.jbs.cam.ac.uk/wp-content/uploads/2020/09/2020-ccaf-3rd-global-cryptoasset-benchmarking-study.pdf?v=1600941674

Board of Governors Department of Securities and of the Treasury Exchange Commission Federal Reserve System. "Joint Report on the Government Securities Market," January 1992. https://www.treasury.gov/resource-center/fin-mkts/Documents/gsr92rpt.pdf

Bordo, Michael D., and Robert N. McCauley. "Triffin: Dilemma or Myth?" *BIS Working Papers*, no. 684. Monetary and Economic Department, Bank of International Settlements, December 2017. https://www.bis.org/publ/work684.pdf

Bowsher, Norman N. "Repurchase Agreements" Federal Reserve Bank of St. Louis. September 1979. https://files.stlouisfed.org/files/htdocs/publications/review/79/09/Repurchase_Sep1979.pdf

Broadbent, Ben (Deputy Governor for Monetary Policy, Bank of England). Speech on "Central Banks and Digital Currencies," presented at the London School of Economics, March 2, 2016. https://www.bankofengland.co.uk/speech/2016/central-banks-and-digital-currencies

Carlos, Ann M. and Larry Neal. "Amsterdam and London as Financial Centers in the Eighteenth Century," *Financial History Review*, vol. 18, issue 1, 2011.

Carney, Mark (Governor of the Bank of England). Speech on "The Growing Challenges for Monetary Policy in the Current International Monetary and Financial System," Jackson Hole Symposium, August 23, 2019. https://www.bankofengland.co.uk/-/media/boe/files/speech/2019/the-growing-challenges-for-monetary-policy-speech-by-mark-carney.pdf

Chen, Justin and Andrew Gibson. "Insights from the Federal Reserve's Weekly Balance Sheet, 1914–1941," *Studies in Applied Economics*, no. 73, 2017. Johns Hopkins Institute for Applied Economics, Global Health, and Study of Business Enterprise.

Ehrenberg, Richard. *Capital and Finance in the Age of the Renaissance*, London: Jonathan Cape, 1928.

Federal Reserve Act, H.R. 7837, 1913.

Federal Reserve Bank of Richmond. "The Gold Cover," *Monthly Review*, The Federal National Mortgage Assn., Fifth District Ports-Virginia, The Fifth District, July 1968. https://fraser.stlouisfed.org/files/docs/publications/frbrichreview/rev_frbrich196807.pdf

Ferguson, Niall. *The Ascent of Money: A Financial History of the World*. New York: Penguin Books, 2009.

Fleming, Michael J., and Klagge, Nicholas J. "The Federal Reserve's Foreign Exchange Swap Lines," in *Economics and Finance*, vol. 16, no. 4, April 2010. Federal Reserve Bank of New York. https://www.newyorkfed.org/medialibrary/media/research/current_issues/ci16-4.pdf

Friedman, Milton. *Money Mischief: Episodes in Monetary History*. Houghton Mifflin Harcourt, 1994.

Friedman, Milton. "The Euro-dollar Market: Some First Principles." Federal Reserve Bank of St Louis, July 1971. https://research.stlouisfed.org/publications/review/1971/07/01/the-euro-dollar-market-some-first-principles/

Fries, Nicholas. "Insights from the Federal Reserve's Weekly Balance Sheet, 1976–2017." *Studies in Applied Economics*, no. 114, 2018. Johns Hopkins Institute for Applied Economics, Global Health, and the Study of Business Enterprise.

Gleeson-White, Jane. *Double Entry: How the Merchants of Venice Created Modern Finance.* New York: W. W. Norton & Company, 2012.

Gold Coins of the Middle Ages. Deutsche Bundesbank Collection. Frankfurt, Germany. https://www.bundesbank.de/resource/blob/607696/f54b6ee83efd2f79e35c9af6e9a3702d/mL/gold-coins-of-the-middle-ages-data.pdf

Goldthwaite, Richard A. *The Economy of Renaissance Florence.* Maryland: Johns Hopkins University Press, 2009.

Grossman, Richard S. "The Origins of Banking," in *Unsettled Account: The Evolution of Banking in the Industrialized World since 1800.* New Jersey: Princeton University Press, 2010. https://www.jstor.org/stable/j.ctt7sw7z.7

Harari, Yuval N. *Sapiens: A Brief History of Humankind.* New York: Harper, 2015.

Harris, Everette B. (President, Chicago Mercantile Exchange). "History of the Chicago Mercantile Exchange." 1970. https://legacy.farmdoc.illinois.edu/irwin/archive/books/Futrs_Tradng_in_Livestck/Futures_Trading_in_%20Livestock_Part%20I_2.pdf

Hearing before the Committee on Banking and Financial Services U.S. House of Representatives, One Hundred Fifth, Second Session, October 1, 1998. https://fraser.stlouisfed.org/title/policy-discussion-papers-federal-reserve-bank-cleveland-4514/lessons-rescue-long-term-capital-management-495652/fulltext

Hearings before the Joint Economic Committee Congress of the United
States, Eighty-Sixth Congress, First Session, October 26-30, 1959.
https://www.jec.senate.gov/reports/86th%20Congress/Hearings/
Constructive%20Suggestions%20for%20Reconciling%20and%20
Simultaneously%20Obtaining%20the%20Three%20Objectives%20
%28130%29.pdf

Jefferson, Thomas. "Notes on the Establishment of a Money Unit, and of
a Coinage for the United States," 1784. https://founders.archives.gov/
documents/Jefferson/01-07-02-0151-0005

Kindleberger, Charles P. "Power and Money." *The Politics of International
Economics and the Economics of International Politics.* New York: Macmillan,
1970.

Logan, Walter S. "Amendments to the Federal Reserve Act," *The Annals
of the American Academy of Political and Social Science*, vol. 99, Jan. 1922,
The Federal Reserve System–Its Purpose and Work, Jan. 1922: 114–121. Sage
Publications Inc., in association with the American Academy of Political
and Social Science. http://www.jstor.com/stable/1014518

McCusker, John J. "The Demise of Distance: The Business Press and the
Origins of the Information Revolution in the Early Modern Atlantic
World," *The American Historical Review*, vol. 110, no. 2, 2005: 295–321.
https://www.jstor.org/stable/10.1086/531316

Mehrling, Perry. "The Inherent Hierarchy of Money," January 25, 2012.
https://ieor.columbia.edu/files/seasdepts/industrial-engineering-opera-
tions-research/pdf-files/Mehrling_P_FESeminar_Sp12-02.pdf

Mehrling, Perry. *The New Lombard Street: How the Fed Became the Dealer of Last Resort.* New Jersey: Princeton University Press, 2010.

Murau, Steffen. "Offshore Dollar Creation and the Emergence of the Post-2008 International Monetary System," IASS Discussion Paper, June 2018. Harvard University — Weatherhead Center for International Affairs; Institute for Advanced Sustainability Studies (IASS). https://publications.iass-potsdam.de/rest/items/item_3259914_4/component/file_3259926/content

Nakamoto, Satoshi. "Bitcoin: A Peer-to-Peer Electronic Cash System." https://bitcoin.org/bitcoin.pdf

Nakamoto Institute. "The Complete Satoshi," 2008-2012. https://satoshi.nakamotoinstitute.org/

Office of the Comptroller of the Currency. Interpretive Letter 1174, "OCC Chief Counsel's Interpretation on National Bank and Federal Savings Association Authority to Use Independent Node Verification Networks and Stablecoins for Payment Activities," January 2021. https://www2.occ.gov/news-issuances/news-releases/2021/nr-occ-2021-2a.pdf

Odell, Kerry, and Marc D. Weidenmier (Working Paper). "Real Shock, Monetary Aftershock: The 1906 San Francisco Earthquake and the Panic of 1907," Claremont Colleges Working Papers in Economics, no. 2001-07. https://www.jstor.org/stable/3874987

Padgett, John F. "Country as Global Market: Netherlands, Calvinism, and the Joint-Stock Company," in *The Emergence of Organizations and Markets Book*, authors John F. Padgett, and Walter W. Powell, New Jersey: Princeton University Press, 2012. http://www.jstor.com/stable/j. cttir2fmz.15

Pozsar, Zoltan. "Shadow Banking: The Money View," Office of Financial Research, U.S. Treasury Department, 2014. https://www.finan-cialresearch.gov/working-papers/files/OFRwp2014-04_Pozsar_ ShadowBankingTheMoneyView.pdf

Quinn, Stephen, and William Roberds. "The Bank of Amsterdam and the Leap to Central Bank Money," *The American Economic Review*, vol. 97, no. 2, 2007: 262–265. https://www.jstor.org/stable/30034457

Quinn, Stephen and William Roberds. "Death of a Reserve Currency," Texas Christian University, Federal Reserve Bank of Atlanta. https://www. frbatlanta.org/-/media/documents/research/publications/wp/2014/wp1417. pdf

Rickards, James. *Currency Wars: The Making of the Next Global Crisis*. Portfolio, 2012.

Roberds, William, and François R. Velde. "The Descent of Central Banks (1400–1815)," Federal Reserve Banks of Atlanta and Chicago, May 27, 2014.

Romer, Christina D. and David H. Romer. "A Rehabilitation of Monetary Policy in the 1950s, Working Paper 8800," *NBER Working Paper Series*, National Bureau of Economic Research, 2002. http://www.nber.org/papers/w8800

Rothbard, Murray N. *History of Money and Banking in the United States: The Colonial Era to World War II*. Ludwig von Mises Institute, 2010.

Schubert, Eric S. "Innovations, Debts, and Bubbles: International Integration of Financial Markets in Western Europe, 1688-1720," *The Journal of Economic History*, vol. 48, no. 2, 1988, *The Tasks of Economic History* June 1988: 299-306. Cambridge University Press on behalf of the Economic History Association. http://www.jstor.com/stable/2121172

Slivinski, Stephen. "Too Interconnected to Fail?" *The Rescue of Long-Term Capital Management*, Region Focus, Federal Reserve Bank of Richmond, Summer 2009. https://www.richmondfed.org/-/media/richmondfedorg/publications/research/econ_focus/2009/summer/pdf/economic_history.pdf

Steil, Benn. *The Battle of Bretton Woods: John Maynard Keynes, Harry Dexter White, and the Making of a New World Order*. Princeton University Press, 2014.

Szabo, Nick. "Shelling Out: The Origins of Money," 2002. https://nakamoto-institute.org/shelling-out/

Taleb, Nassim. *Antifragile: Things That Gain from Disorder*. Random House, 2012.

Triffin, Robert. "Gold and the Dollar Crisis: Yesterday and Tomorrow," *Essays in International Finance*, no. 132, December 1978. https://ies.princeton.edu/pdf/E132.pdf

United States Court of Appeals, Ninth Circuit. *Daniel J. Bernstein v. United States Department of State et al*, 1997. https://caselaw.findlaw.com/us-9th-circuit/1317290.html

Weber, Warren E. "Government and Private E-Money-Like Systems: Federal Reserve Notes and National Bank Notes," *CenFIS Working Paper*, 15-03, August 2015. Federal Reserve Bank of Atlanta. https://www.frbatlanta.org/-/media/documents/cenfis/publications/wp/2015/1503.pdf

Wee, Herman Van der. "Globalization, Core, and Periphery in the World Economy in the Late Middle Ages and Early Modern Times," in *Cores, Peripheries, and Globalization*, edited by Peter Hans Reill and Balázs A. Szelényi. Central European University Press, 2011. http://www.jstor.com/stable/10.7829/j.ctt1282x8.14

Wee, Herman Van der. "International Business Finance and Monetary Policy in Western Europe, 1384-1410," *The Business History Review*, vol. 43, no. 3, Autumn 1969: 372–380. http://www.jstor.com/stable/3112388

World Economic Forum. "Insight Report, Central Bank Digital Currency Policy-Maker Toolkit," Centre for the Fourth Industrial Revolution, 2020. http://www3.weforum.org/docs/WEF_CBDC_Policymaker_Toolkit.pdf

ABOUT THE AUTHOR

NIK BHATIA is a financial researcher, CFA charterholder, and Adjunct Professor of Finance and Business Economics at the University of Southern California Marshall School of Business where he teaches Applied Finance in Fixed Income Securities. Previously, Nik worked the US Treasuries trading desk for a large institutional asset manager and has extensive trading experience in money markets and interest rate futures. After starting his teaching career, Nik felt the urge to bring his research on both the international monetary system and Bitcoin together as one to write *Layered Money: From Gold and Dollars to Bitcoin and Central Bank Digital Currencies.* He has a BA in Social Sciences from University of Southern California and a Master in Finance from IE Business School in Madrid, Spain. Nik lives in Los Angeles, CA with his wife and young daughter.

LAYERED**MONEY**.COM